This book takes a creative and
the makeover. Many times, it's
doesn't stop with the visible. She helps women to learn to be their best on the
outside, while also speaking an even greater message: true beauty and significance
flow out of a vibrant and healthy relationship with God.

Glamour Girl: How To Get The Ultimate Makeover is a great "how-to" guide that
will inspire women to be their best inside and out.

— PASTOR JOHN SIEBELING
The Life Church
www.thelifechurch.com

In her book, *Glamour Girl,* Megan Mottley describes the true meaning of beauty,
biblically speaking. In 1 Peter 3:3, Peter said, "Your beauty should not come from
outward adornment...v 4) Instead, it should be that of your inner self, of unfading
beauty of the gentle and quiet spirit, which is of great worth in God's sight."

Megan has strategically outlined all of the principles in the word of God, and in
daily living, of how to reach the ultimate inward beauty. This read is a must for
young ladies, and women who are seeking a deeper and closer relationship with
our heavenly Father, and becoming all that He has destined for our lives.

— JUDY JACOBS
His Song Ministries
www.judyjacobs.com

Megan nails it! This book is required reading for all women. As for the men,
you must have a copy to speak to the internal beauty of your wife, girlfriend or
significant other.

— DERRICK MILES
Chairman/CEO of The Milestone Brand
www.milestonebrand.com

There is nothing more beautiful than someone who appears elegant, confident and effortless on the outside, and then you discover she has an even greater inner beauty, strength and spirituality. Megan Mottley, a true glamour girl herself is the inspirational "beauty consultant" for any and every woman in *Glamour Girl: How To Get The Ultimate Makeover*. Her guidebook is a must read for women who need a reminder that she is ultimately beautiful especially when she makes God a part of her life.

— TRAN BUI SMITH
Award-Winning TV Journalist/Co-Creator of Nationally-Televised
Show Traveling with Tots
www.travelingwithtots.info

If we want to live in The Blessing, we must do as the Lord instructs us in Isaiah 55, and exchange our thoughts for His thoughts. In her book, Megan takes the reader through a well-laid-out process of thought exchange. She brilliantly explains why God wants women to be kingdom thinkers — BIG thinkers — and not poor-minded worriers or women of shallow existence! Megan challenges, inspires, and ignites women to change their way of thinking and to start walking boldly in their purpose. For the woman who is ready to improve her relationships, heal her heart and reach total success, this is the right book for the journey! More than hope and inspiration, this book offers a template for victory and serves as a roadmap to move past previous blocks. Megan's book is a "beauty tool" that every *true* Glamour Girl should have!

— JEWEL TANKARD
Co-Pastor of Destiny Center
www.thedestinydome.com

When I received Megan's manuscript, *Glamour Girl: How To Get The Ultimate Makeover*, being a man, I felt a bit unqualified to objectively review what I at first assumed to be a book of "how to look beautiful" for women. As I began to read this work, I quickly discovered that God has given Megan a unique revelation of far more than the art of applying *cosmetic aesthetics*.

I have never seen a book of this kind. Megan brilliantly weaves in biblical truths as she defines the fundamentals of a basic makeover. Comparing and contrasting the steps of this process, and their spiritual correlations, such as cleansing, proper foundation, etc., is not only avant-garde; but even more, an absolutely relevant way to share the gospel with young women who live in a culture that worships the idol of image.

Megan incorporates the story of Esther and her flawless character that shined even brighter than her outward beauty, as she rose to the challenge of rescuing a nation from certain death. I was so touched by this work that I have made it a mandatory read for my 14 and 15 year old daughters, as it steps into the world they live in every morning as they get ready for school and speaks truth to them in a way that their father never could!

I am so proud of Megan and this book is a critical read for any female at any age!

— JONATHAN S. POTTER
Author – *Spiritual Identity Fraud: Restoring God's Sons and Daughters*
www.jonpotterministries.net

Glamour Girl: How To Get The Ultimate Makeover cleverly strips off layers of self-doubt and, in many cases, self-loathing. In the process, it reveals how God sees us and how we should view ourselves. Megan Mottley uses scripture to apply a gentle cleanser that removes the residue of past imperfections and is safe for every complexion. The biblical stories apply just the right toner to enhance and brighten areas that have been darkened by life's circumstances. The end product is an enlightened woman who is made over for God's glory and good.

— DEE GRIFFIN
Television News Anchor and Reporter

Glamour Girl
How To Get The
Ultimate Makeover

Megan Mottley

MTLY
PUBLISHING HOUSE
A Division of MTLY Communications

Most MTLY COMMUNICATIONS/MTLY PUBLISHING HOUSE products are available at special quantity discounts for bulk purchase for sales promotions, fundraising, premiums, and educational needs. For details, write MTLY Communications/MTLY Publishing, 6801 Summer Avenue, Suite 102, Bartlett, TN 38134 or call (855) 456-4475.

GLAMOUR GIRL: HOW TO GET THE ULTIMATE MAKEOVER
by Megan Mottley
Published by MTLY PUBLISHING
A Division of MTLY Communications
6801 Summer Avenue, Suite 102
Bartlett, TN 38134
www.mtlycommunications.com

Cover Design by Tiffany Lambert of Tart Design. Olive Branch, Mississippi

GLAMOUR GIRL: HOW TO GET THE ULTIMATE MAKEOVER
Copyright © 2011 by Megan Mottley
Published by MTLY Books & Publishing
Bartlett, TN 38134
www.mtlycommunications.com

ISBN 978-0-615-56137-0

Library of Congress Control Number: 2011919864

MTLY Publishing is a division of MTLY Communications.

Printed in the United States of America

Dedication

To women who need to be reminded of their worth,

their purpose and their beauty. You have what

it takes to be a True Glamour Girl —

one who embraces beauty from the inside

out and walks boldly in her purpose.

To the people who never let me quit.

Acknowledgments

To my family

Jerry, Beatrice, Torrie, Jerriey

You have been there with me through all of the ups and downs, the trials and tribulations, the smiles, the tears, the mountaintop experiences and the valley experiences. I couldn't have made it without you. It is because of your faith in me that I have written and published my first book. This book is dedicated to you.

To my precious daughter

Kaitlin

You are the most beautiful, intelligent, sweet, and patient daughter that anyone can ask for. I live for you. I work endless hours, push forward through brick walls and jump over obstacles because of you — so I can be an example to you. I hope that you are pleased with the finished product and that my hard work will inspire you for years to come.

*To the entire Mottley family, the Boyd family, my friends,
the ladies of Delta Sigma Theta Sorority, Inc. (Epsilon Kappa
Chapter), my church family (New Salem, New Bethel, Life Church),
my Life Coach Khama Anku, my Editor L. Marie Harris, my
assistant Jessica Bailey, my IIOM family (esp. Pastor Judy Jacobs,
Pastor Jamie Tuttle, Dr. Sheila Cornea), the Faculty and Staff of
the University of Memphis Journalism and MALS Department,
the Mastermind Group of Memphis, Tonya Hilson and the Women
With Vision Group and the countless others who played a part in
helping to create this book.*

You have all shaped me in some way and I appreciate
you for your support over the years.

*To my Glam Squad
Jonathan Nelson (Jo'V), Atlantis White, Bryant-Joshua Perry,
Quinest Bishop, Tiffany Lambert, Courtney Long*

Thank you so much for helping me to bring my Glamour
Girl Movement vision to fruition. Together you all did a
magnificent job of making me look GLAMOROUS on
the cover and the official website.

*To those of you who told me I could when I thought that
I couldn't, who prayed over me when I thought all hope was
gone, who pushed me to recognize that I had a gift inside of me,
who have looked up to me and given me a reason to share my
experiences so that we all can live a life that is pleasing
to our Creator. I'm grateful for you.*
I love you.

Glamour Girl Prayer

Lord, I pray for each woman connected to the Glamour Girl Movement. I pray that she will receive everything that you would have her to receive from the pages of this book and this movement. I pray that the Glamour Girl Movement and *Glamour Girl: How To Get The Ultimate Makeover* is a huge blessing to every woman who desires to find the true glamour girl that exists within. For each woman who reads this book, I pray that you will order her steps and show her the purpose for which she was created. Lord, use my words as a catalyst to ignite the fire of beauty from the inside out of each and every reader. I pray that *Glamour Girl: How To Get The Ultimate Makeover* and the Glamour Girl Movement will inspire women everywhere to be what you have called them to be no matter where they've been or what they've done.

Lord, we give you the honor and the glory and we thank you for loving us through each and every phase of our lives.

Amen.

—Megan Mottley, Author
Founder and Creator of the Glamour Girl Movement
www.theglamourgirlmovement.com

Contents

Foreword

When Megan asked me to write a foreword for her book I was certainly up for the task but not without some hesitation as to what message I would convey to women on the subject of beauty. As I came to understand more of what The Glamour Girl Movement was about and the subject of this book, it became clear to me why there was indeed a profound message for women to grasp about beauty.

A few years ago, I vividly remember talking to Megan a short time after she had given birth to her daughter. She was searching for direction in life and I was determined to help her to see that she had reached a pivotal stage in her life. It was important for me to explain to Megan that she could either continue down a road of uncertainty, pain and frustration or set foot on a path that would lead straight to what God had already predestined. I encouraged Megan to take a sabbatical; to spend some serious alone time with God, focus on her daughter and get back on track. I am not surprised that Megan, being the young woman of faith that she is, would be so impacted by the results of her sabbatical that she would write an entire book to inspire others to do the same.

Megan, like any other person, has encountered the ups and downs of life but with the right attitude, a support system like no other and faith for the journey, she pressed through her trials and emerged as a true *Glamour Girl*.

Megan has written not only an interesting book but a great book on a very difficult and debatable subject — BEAUTY. The mystery of attractiveness and beauty has almost been a lifelong human search. It is said that many of us spend approximately one-third of our income on looking good. Probably at the basis of this mystery and controversy is Margaret Wolf Hungerford's statement — "Beauty is in the eye of the beholder."

Megan makes this diverse subject both intriguing and simple because she places the subject matter under the literary microscope and magnifies it so as to appeal to the holistic being of the readers — the emotional, the psychological and the spiritual (1 Thess. 5:23).

Psychologist Dr. Vivian Diller directs the right questions to the right gender and brings us to what Godly beauty really is. Two questions should be asked and answered:

What makes women look attractive (from a male perspective)?

What makes women feel attractive (from a female perspective)?

Men ranked a great smile first as the quality that made a woman of any age look beautiful to them. Good skin, long hair, a voluptuous body, great legs and good posture were also mentioned. Older men seemed to focus more on the physical aspects of beauty seen on women's faces, while younger men talked more about women's bodies.

Now — what makes women feel attractive (from a female perspective)? Instead of youthful looks, the quality that was most often cited by women when it comes to feeling attractive was appearing genuinely happy. And this was true for women of all ages. The shift from looking to feeling attractive moved women from the external to the internal, from a focus on the physical to the positive feelings that made them attractive to themselves.

Godly beauty can be dualistically manifested. This concept unfolds clearly and more majestically powerful in Genesis 24 than any place else. Abraham's servant found his master's son Isaac a bride — as it turns out, Rebekah was very beautiful to look upon (Gen. 24:15-16). She was not only good looking; she was very polite, courteous, and possessed inward beauty (Gen. 24:17-19). Abraham's servant picked her because of both aspects of her beauty. The Puritans thought that beauty was of the devil. He is beautiful. He is an angel of light (2 Cor. 11:14), but he does not have all the beauty. God created the sunset and the beautiful flowers, and He's the one who makes women beautiful too. My perspective on Godly beauty will continue to be a study of aesthetics, sociology, social psychology, and culture. Therefore, let's consider a 45-year-old rock-and-roll song written by Norman Whitfield and Edward Holland: "Beauty Is Only Skin Deep," a 1966 hit single recorded by The Temptations. After reflecting on the lyrics of this song, one would have to agree that the message of Godly beauty is clear: she may not have a pretty face, but her inward qualities take over his heart. He not only falls in love, he stays in love with her.

Megan's personal honesty and thorough approach guides the serious reader to the Ultimate Makeover. And since self-evaluation opens the door to self-discovery and self-discovery to self-improvement — this book invites its readers to be self-critical — which is to stand on the very threshold of Godly beauty.

—*Dr. Earnest Mottley, D.Min.*
Pastor of Springhill M.B. Church

Introduction

After bearing a child out of wedlock, I had totally lost all perspective for my purpose and God's will for my life. Long after God had forgiven me and long after friends and family embraced me with words of encouragement and hope for the future, I still hadn't found a way to forgive myself. A close uncle, who is also a minister, suggested that I take a sabbatical for a year to regain perspective of my relationship with God. He also instructed me to take time to build a solid foundation with my daughter. A sabbatical is in a sense a form of fasting but in essence it's time alone with God, critically reading scripture and being available for God to use you. During this time my heart and my mind were open to receive a profound message from God. I became fascinated with the Book of Esther and why she and several other women had to encounter 12 months of purification — a requirement of King Ahasuerus who was in search of a new queen. I thought that it was very fascinating that I was going through a 12-month process similar to that of Esther. I set out to discover exactly what Esther and the other women had to endure for an entire year and why. I also began to compare these biblical discoveries with modern day beauty treatments and the use of cosmetics. I saw the need to bring the Book of Esther to life and to show women the purpose of God-Inspired Beauty Secrets. I also wanted to share with women what I discovered about God and myself during my yearlong sabbatical and how setting aside some time to be alone with God whether it is for one month, three months or 12 months can be a very invigorating experience. The purpose of my book is to encourage women to allow God to give them the ultimate makeover. The result is similar to those before and after pictures that are seen in magazines and on television, women will be amazed at the difference.

Glamour Girl Verse

*"And who knows but that you
have come to your royal position
for such a time as this?"*
Esther 4:14 NIV

Chapter 1

It's What's On The Inside

Have you ever seen the before and after photos of a woman who has received a makeover? The before pictures capture a plain and original look. The after pictures capture flawless skin, gorgeous eyes, visible cheekbones, and lips kissed with flattering color. The difference is stunning and captivating. The meaning goes deeper than what the eyes can see. The purpose is to show the dramatics of allowing oneself to go through a beauty regimen under the care of a professional and being more than pleased with the results. You should know exactly what I'm talking about because either you or someone you know has experienced a makeover. However, have you ever had the ultimate makeover by the Master to the pros? Have you ever once thought about how you could allow God to make you over? The results could make all the difference in your life and the lives of others. The makeup that we put on our faces to achieve instant beauty results is no comparison to the values and experiences that God can place in our lives to achieve eternal benefits. We can however learn a valuable lesson from the purpose of makeup and how we use it.

Before we delve into the wonderful world of makeup, let's pause to focus on what I consider the most beautiful sight on this earth — a well-kept woman. From head to toe she exudes confidence, power, strength and femininity all wrapped up into one package. When you see her you think, "Wow, she is beautiful." You secretly wonder what you can do to resemble that type of beauty. Notice I didn't mention anything about her outer garments or other enhancements. External beauty is a gift from God but internal beauty is the most important type of beauty to God. If God has blessed you with external beauty it definitely should not supersede your inner beauty — it should complement it. "You should not use outward aids to make yourselves beautiful, such as the way you fix your hair, or the jewelry you put on, or the dresses you wear. Instead, your beauty should consist of your true inner self, the ageless beauty of a gentle and quiet spirit, which is of the greatest value in God's sight" (I Pet. 3: 3-4 TEV). This text is not saying that you shouldn't take the time to enhance your physical features but it is saying do not let these things validate you or represent your entire worth. It is inner beauty that should shine forth above any "outward aid." In short, the more beauty a woman has, especially internally, the more she pleases God and the more her life affects others. Above all, if her life falls in line with the will of God, that kind of beauty is never vain.

What Matters Most

As women we spend time trying to please God and the opposite sex. Men see our outer beauty first and so we focus on illuminating our outer appearance as much as possible. Not only do we aim to please men but we also want to look the part for church, work, social events and basically wherever we go. All of this is worthless if we as women do not understand what matters most to God. The description of a virtuous woman in Proverbs 31 does not go without mentioning beauty; however, beauty is not necessarily associated with virtue. Much to the reader's surprise, Proverbs 31 does not mention anything about this virtuous woman's physical features. It is possible that she was drop dead gorgeous but was that important to mention? Or is it more vital to note how much faith her husband had in her, or how she was business minded, or how she helped the needy? What about how she took good care of her family, how they blessed and praised her constantly, or how she spoke with wisdom and kindness? Being able to woo people with charm and good looks does not make a woman virtuous. It can however limit her ability to serve God and others. "Favor is deceitful, and beauty is vain, but a woman that feareth the Lord, she shall be praised" (Prov. 31:30). I believe that the virtuous woman mentioned in Proverbs 31 was very beautiful, don't you?

The Most Beautiful Thing

As women we should all be aware of the qualities that give us inner beauty like self-esteem, determination, kindness, patience, confidence, sensitivity and so on. We may not exactly possess all of these qualities but like the fruit of the Spirit these things take time to grow and develop in us. The Bible mentions traits such as "love, joy, peace, long-suffering, gentleness, goodness, faith, meekness, [and] temperance" and these traits do not develop overnight but over time (Gal. 5:22-23). So how do we allow the fruit of the Spirit to develop in our lives? It is really plain and simple. We must first be in a relationship with God. He says, "abide in me, and I in you. As the branch cannot bear fruit of itself, except it abide in the vine; no more can ye, except ye abide in me" (John 15:4). You cannot expect the fruit of the Spirit to grow in your life if you are disconnected from the vine, which metaphorically is Jesus. So in order to stay connected to Jesus we must live with Him, eat with Him, talk with Him and even get ready for our day with Him. We must do these things so that He can live with us, eat with us, talk with us and get *us* ready for our day. If not, we're just living and breathing without any type of support system from God. Living in this manner will cause us to shrivel up and die right along with our relationships with others and most importantly the ministries to which God has called us.

The Bible goes on to say that if we abide in Jesus and He abides in us that whatever we ask for shall come to pass. Sometimes it is hard to uphold the fruit of the Spirit when someone has stabbed you in the back or someone cuts you off on the road or your reputation has been tainted at work. Sometimes I think if I didn't know right from wrong, I could get away with seeking a little revenge. In spite of all the wishful thinking, the most beautiful thing in this world is knowing that the harder I work at possessing qualities of inner beauty, the closer that I will grow to God and remain one of His disciples. Jesus said, "ye are my friends, if ye do whatsoever I command you" (John 15:14) and I cannot think of any better friend than that. They say diamonds are a girl's best friend but I beg to differ because God is truly a woman's best friend; He can give you diamonds and then some!

The Ultimate Makeover

God is speaking to Christian women everywhere about how He can give them the ultimate makeover. It is high time that Christian women slow down long enough to take a real deep look in the mirror. Not just to check to see if a hair is out of place or if our lipstick needs a touch-up. I'm talking about a spiritual look in the mirror. You may be dealing with skeletons in your closet or you may even be premeditating a moment to ruin someone's marriage because that's what happened to you. Your life might be filled with more downs than ups or you might be dealing with a serious case of loneliness and you've got people all around you. Whatever the case, it is time to whip out that spiritual mirror and begin self-evaluation.

My experience of bearing a child out of wedlock and becoming a single mother caused me to take my first look into the spiritual mirror. Taking a look at myself through the eyes of God certainly helped me to have much better judgment and to be more sensitive to His word. So while I might not be the most ideal source, based on my past excursions, I am a credible source. Fortunately Jesus does not discriminate against anyone based on their past. He always has open arms for each of us no matter what. "But the pot he was shaping from the clay was marred in his hands; so the potter formed it into another pot, shaping it as seemed best to him" (Jer. 18:4 NIV). Jesus is always there to make the best out of the situation whenever we fall short. He always knows how to "shape" us into our purpose even when we fall by the wayside.

I urge you to steal away from the pressures of life and analyze where you are, where you've been and where you're going. Like the words to a familiar Diana Ross song, "Do you know where you're going to, do you like the things that life is showing you?" If you don't like what you see in your spiritual mirror, won't you allow God to give you the ultimate makeover?

Chapter 2

Life-Changing Beauty Secrets

The alarm rings at 6:15 a.m. Simone awakes to begin a new day and silently thanks God for the opportunity. Among her daily morning rituals, the most exciting moment that she embraces is the time that she takes to put on her makeup. Simone is usually impressed with the results and enjoys her chance to express her uniqueness of character with her small but significant quantity of makeup. Whether she's feeling a little glamorous with eye catching shades or just wanting to keep it natural with earth tones, Simone often mirrors her mood through her beauty rituals. If it's a slow morning, Simone can easily lift her frame of mind by mimicking something that she saw in her favorite magazine. If she wants to make a huge impression on a prospective client, Simone boosts her confidence by painting on her very best professional face. Whatever the case, Simone enjoys being able to tap into a side of herself that can reveal what she is feeling or she can choose to keep her feelings hidden if only for a while. The clock now reads 7:45 a.m. and Simone is out the door to face the world head on.

If you're like Simone, you dab on a little makeup to enhance your facial features before you dash off to church, work or even to the mall. It's nothing out of the ordinary and is just a way to feel better about you. You may go for a natural look or you may choose to illuminate your eyes and lips with a shade that coordinates with the outfit that you're wearing. If you have the products and the time then you are free to be whoever you want to be for a day. You have the power to change your mood, your facial features and much more. You have the power to change your life. You may be thinking, "Makeup surely can't do all of that." Well it can, especially from a spiritual point of view. With God all things are possible and when you get closer and closer to Him you start to look at things that you once took for granted on a much deeper level. Each step associated with applying makeup can be expounded upon in a spiritual realm. Brace yourself because you are about to encounter some of the most life-changing beauty secrets ever!

Beauty Basics

Every good painter knows that starting with a smooth canvas is beneficial to achieving a lasting masterpiece of beautiful artwork. Every good makeup artist knows that starting with clean and healthy skin is vital in order to create a flawless picture of beauty. The more precise you are in your efforts to apply makeup, the better the outcome of the entire process. You don't have to be a professional makeup artist to know that makeup should be applied to the skin in a neat and orderly fashion. The Bible says, "Let all things be done decently and in order" (I Cor. 14:40) so why skip a beat here? Starting with clean skin is essential and without a doubt a wise thing to do. It doesn't make any sense to apply makeup to skin that has not been properly prepared. Okay? So how do you prepare the skin properly? You must follow three very important steps:

1) Cleanse

2) Tone

3) Moisturize

This may sound strange but think about all of the oil, dirt and debris that has come into contact with your skin from your hair, hands, nails, telephone receivers, etc. When you cleanse you remove most of the debris on your skin, the toner picks up the excess and the moisturizer rejuvenates the skin, eliminates dryness and protects the skin against harmful sun damage.

If you fail to properly prepare your skin prior to adding makeup then you are more susceptible to blackheads, whiteheads, etc. We all should remember this from high school and for some of us it is still a problem from time to time. So the keyword here is "prepare."

Pep Talk

Now I realize that we don't get up every single morning wanting to put on makeup. Some mornings all I feel like putting on is a dab of lip balm and I'm out the door. Other mornings I feel like splurging and I take the time to spruce up a little bit more. The following steps are not meant to make you feel like this must be an everyday routine. So without further delay, let's prepare our hearts and minds and set the mood.

You have been asked to speak at a women's conference in your city and your topic is *Self-Image and Its Benefits,* so of course you don't want to show up looking like a vagabond. You have your outfit and accessories together as well as your speech. On top of that your hair is picture perfect and since your best friend is a professional makeup artist, she's about to turn you into America's Next Top Model.

So let's pretend that I'm the best friend and the makeup artist. This is where I step in to offer you some meaningful tips on makeup application as well as a few points to encourage spiritual growth. The key to remember is that as Christian women everything that we do should be pleasing to God and in this case it's makeup. Now, let's get started!

Primer

There's nothing more important than starting with the end in mind. As it relates to makeup, the best way to achieve lasting results and ensure that every product that you apply looks professional and picture perfect is to start the makeup application process with a primer. The main benefit of primer is that it forms a bond with all of your cosmetic products to hold your look better and longer. Primers come in different textures, some contain moisture-enriching vitamins and others contain botanicals that fight off the aging process. Primers also serve different purposes, for example, lip primers help to slow down the fading process of your lipstick and keep your lip colors fresh while eye shadow primers help your shadows go on smoothly and eliminate creasing. Primers designed for the entire skin surface can be colorless or tinted and can often cut down on the amount of foundation used, saving you money in the long run.

From oily skin to dry skin, primer serves to prepare the skin to look its best and feel its best. By using primer, you are setting your skin up for success and you are setting the tone for how well your makeup will look at the end of the day. If you've never used primer, it's time to step up your makeup game. You may be very surprised at how a little preparation can go a long way. It may seem like one extra step or a step that you never knew existed but the results will be remarkable and the compliments will be non-stop.

Just as primer helps to prepare the skin, it is a must that you allow the concept of preparation to permeate into your soul. When you take the time to prepare for something, the end results are nothing short of amazing. Think about the last time that you prepared for a test — the time you took to study, to meet with your study group and even to ask your professor for guidance. I'm sure that you would agree that in the end, all of the preparations that you made to succeed paid off. Likewise, whatever you're preparing for, be it a new career, a husband, a child, a new home, a new car, etc., the fact that you're taking the time to prepare makes you a cut above the rest.

Being prepared for every opportunity that comes along is a trait of a virtuous woman. "She gets up while it is still night... She watches over the affairs of her household and does not eat the bread of idleness" (Proverbs 31: 15, 27 NIV). The virtuous woman takes time to prepare for her daily activities, for her family, for her business, etc. She values her time and everyone else's time and she eliminates the added stress that comes along with unpreparedness.

Make it a point to *prepare* for your sacred time with God. In order to fully hear from God and be in tune to what He has destined for your future, you have to spend time in your Word, remain under divine teaching and constantly walk in Godly principles. God is your Creator, so who better to have a strong relationship with in order to discover the best route for your life. Just as you would use primer to prep your skin for full day coverage, also prepare diligently to use the gifts that you have inside of you that are supernaturally designed to have a lasting effect on generations.

Foundation

After you apply your primer, the next step is foundation, or base, mainly because it is a must that you create a flawless background. The purpose of foundation is to give the skin's complexion an even look before applying eye shadow, lipstick and other cosmetics.

Many women choose not to wear foundation because they have yet to find the perfect match to their skin tone. We come in all shades and finding the right color can sometimes mean having to mix foundation colors together which can be a nuisance. Another factor that can cause frustration is the unawareness of which texture to choose — liquid, cream, stick or powder.

Here's a quick lesson. Liquid is the most commonly used foundation with the attributes of good coverage, effortless application and a natural look. Cream and stick foundation also provide good coverage but is not recommended for oily skin because it is so heavy in texture. Cake foundation is just what it sounds like: "cake-y," dry and is basically designed for people who work on television or in theatre and required to work under bright lights. Having stated that, the confusion about which type of foundation to use should be a thing of the past. Choose whichever foundation works for you based on your skin type — oily, dry or combination.

> **TIP:** Due to innovations in the makeup industry, sheer tints and tinted moisturizers have also been created and used as substitutes for foundation. So if you're not sure how you would look with foundation or if you want to have a really natural look then sheer tint may be for you.

It's vital to take the time to pick the correct shade of foundation and apply it with precision to achieve maximum results. In the same way, if we build a good foundation in Christ, good people and good things will begin to just fall into place in our lives. Jesus will forgive us of any sins so that we may begin with a flawless background! Not only that, Jesus urged Christians to have a solid foundation by hearing His word. Matthew 7:24-27 teaches about a wise man who built his house upon a rock and the foolish man who built his house upon the sand. The wise man represented someone hearing the Word and doing as it says while the foolish man represented someone hearing the Word but failing to act on it. The bottom line is to follow instructions when you receive them!

Demarcation

One fact that is very important to remember in regard to the end result of foundation is something known to makeup artists as demarcation. This happens around the hairline and at the jaw line and looks like a mask. Demarcation occurs because the makeup isn't blended well and causes a line of separation between the actual skin tone and the color of the foundation. No matter how close the foundation is in color to the skin tone, demarcation can still occur. Always blend your foundation well.

From a spiritual point of view, demarcation is like riding the fence or having one foot in the world and one foot in the church. Either way you don't belong or you don't blend well. Mainly because when you're doing things that are of this world you know that the people you spend time with or the places that you go are not healthy to your spiritual walk. At the same time when you do attend church you can't fully receive God's word because the world has such a stronghold on your heart and your mind. The best thing to do is to choose which way you want to live your life. You can't be lukewarm! It would be unfortunate if God woke us up one day but forgot all about us the rest of the week. Regardless of how we neglect God, we want Him smiling on us all the days of our lives. The time has come for us to give God what's due to Him for all the blessings that He has bestowed upon us. The only way to make strides toward fully loving and honoring God is to have two feet in the church or your place of worship and make sure your relationship with God is in full force. Go ahead, blend in with your fellow worshippers, servers and followers of Christ.

For Best Results

So what have we learned so far? We have learned to start with a good foundation and blend it well. It is also important to check often for oily spots, dry spots, or just to touch-up. All of these components will help you to achieve the best results from your foundation.

To take it a step further, always listen to the advice of professionals on techniques and procedures. Read magazine articles and books to learn as much as possible. Also peruse the Internet for a plethora of video tutorials. Stay up on the latest trends and products. Although some techniques and products are tried and true, innovations in these areas can save time and money.

When it comes to your relationship with God you also want to achieve the best results. Get a good foundation by reading His word daily, meditating on it and applying it to your life. Fellowship with other believers and let your testimony bless someone else. Do all that you can to stay close to God and to share His goodness to people everywhere. Don't straddle the fence, do your best to blend well with Christ by acting and doing as He would. Lastly, touch-up on your foundation with Christ often checking for areas in your life that need a new application of His mercy and grace. Never forsake the reading of His word because it always has something new that can minister to your soul and the souls of others. When you do these things on a consistent basis you will achieve the best results of a good foundation with Christ.

Let the thought of foundation always remind you of the importance of doing what it takes to stay grounded in God and grounded in life. "But seek first the kingdom of God, and His righteousness, and all these things shall be added to you" (Matt. 6:33 NKJV). Take heed to God's word and receive every blessing that God has in store for you. Build a good foundation and let God "pour you out a blessing, that there shall not be room enough to receive it" (Mal. 3:10).

Face Powder

Now I know you're thinking face powder too! Well don't fret because powder is your friend. It is used to simply set your foundation. Although it can be eliminated, if you have a desire to have a matte finish then you definitely want to use powder, particularly translucent powder.

> **TIP:** Translucent powder doesn't necessarily have a color so it won't change the color of your foundation.

When you skip the step of using face powder you cut down the chances of your makeup lasting as long as it could. Remember, you always want to do what it takes to achieve maximum results.

You don't have to pile a vast amount of powder on your skin. Instead, use a clean brush to lightly dust powder onto your skin or use a sponge to gently press the powder onto the skin concentrating on areas that are susceptible to oil.

You always have the right to eliminate certain steps in applying makeup. However, it doesn't necessarily mean that it's the best way to go about doing things. Skipping a step may save time but it may cost you in the long run. Not only is this true for rules of makeup but it is also true for your day-to-day life, especially in your relationship with God. Just like you may have cringed at the thought of face powder and foundation, we also gripe and complain about things that God knows may seem like a hassle to us but is really an overall grooming process. You may enter a time in our life where God leads you to take on numerous roles in your church or communities just to see if you are capable of following instructions or if you have what it takes to be versatile. He could very well be equipping you to move to another level in life. A level that may prepare you for things that you have been praying for such as marriage, leadership roles, or simple obedience.

You probably think that you could go without being the Vacation Bible School Director when you are already the Sunday School Superintendent but God will always give you double for your trouble in the end. "For our light affliction which is but for a moment, worketh for us a far more exceeding and eternal weight of glory, while we look not at the things which are seen, but at the things which are not seen; for the things which are seen are temporal, but the things which are not seen are eternal" (2 Cor. 4: 17-18).

There's so much value in going that extra mile to please God. It may not be comfortable at first and it may not even be something that you want to do but you owe God your obedience. He can't help

19

but be proud of His obedient child(ren) and ready to express His love for you. He will even work out situations in your life like no other. "When a man's ways please the Lord, he maketh even his enemies to be at peace with him" (Prov. 16:7). Imagine that!

Eye Shadow

Eyes come in all shapes and sizes and can be the most important part of makeup. Eye shadow, which comes in cream, loose or powder forms, enhance the shape and even the color of the eyes. Precision is key when it comes to eye shadow because one error can have a great effect on the overall face. You've seen someone with too much eye shadow or colors that are all wrong for their skin tone or their outfit. Even if everything else is applied perfectly, eye shadow applied wrongly causes major problems for the person as a whole.

You can't talk about eye shadow without talking about eyebrows, which should be kept well groomed by waxing or threading. (I don't recommend razors because this causes ingrown hairs.) Eyebrows frame the eyes to make eye makeup look so much better.

> **TIP:** Use a sharpened eyeliner pencil close to the brow color to fill in spaces in eyebrows if necessary. When using an eyeliner pencil to fill in spaces in your eyebrows be sure to use tiny strokes so that the end result looks natural. You may also use eye shadow that matches your brow to lightly shade in color.

Another important part of eye makeup is eyeliner, which gives sharper definition to the shape of the eye. Eyeliners elongate the eyelashes and even enhance the white of the eye making the eyes look larger. Eyeliners come in pencil, liquid, gel and cake. So if you're not a pro skip the cake, start with a pencil and then graduate to liquid because this step requires a neat finish.

> **TIP:** If you have tiny eyes never line the bottom lid around your eyes because it tends to close up the eyes. If necessary, talk with a makeup professional about eyeliner colors that open up the eyes when used on the bottom lid.

Mascara adds color and effect to eyelashes to emphasize the eyes. The basic colors are black, brown and navy, but innovations in cosmetics have produced every color that you can imagine so don't get too crazy.

> **TIP:** Never share mascara for obvious reasons but mainly for health reasons. Always change mascara every three to six months (yes ladies!) to be on the safe side and to avoid drying and caking, which results in spider legs and ugly clumps.

So remember that eye shadow is your friend. Don't be shy. Experiment with colors but save the deeper tones and glitter accents for night time and use more natural tones for the daytime.

Spiritually, eye shadow represents there being a time and a place for everything. I say this because the wrong shades or the wrong techniques can be very unattractive. Therefore, when applying eye shadow remember that everything has a time and a season in your life. If you were hiring for a position and the applicant came to the interview with glitter eye shadow, how likely would you be to hire her? I'm sure that you would agree that glitter eye shadow is a bit out of place for a job interview and that it would be best to go with colors so natural it's barely there. On that same note, if you're believing God for something (a new job, a new car, a husband, etc.) but the timing isn't right, then you may have to exhibit a little more patience and respect God's timing for bringing things to fruition in your life. So from now on while you're working to get that eye shadow right take some time and think about everything having a time and a place. Remember also what Ecclesiastes 3:1-9 says:

> *To every thing there is a season, and a time to every purpose under the heaven: A time to be born, and a time to die; a time to plant, and a time to pluck up that which is planted; A time to kill, and a time to heal; a time to break down, and a time to build up; A time to weep, and a time to laugh; a time to mourn, and a time to dance; A time to cast away stones, and a time to gather stones together; a time to embrace, and a time to refrain from embracing; A time to get, and a time to lose; a time to keep, and a time to cast away; A time to rend, and a time to sew; a time to keep silence, and a time to speak; A time to love, and a time to hate; a time of war, and a time of peace.*

Lastly, with all this focus on the eyes it would be a tragedy not to mention the importance of shielding our eyes from wickedness. I'm sure you remember that song "Oh be careful little eyes what you see." Well that song is so true, even as adults we need to be mindful of how important our eyes are to our bodies as a whole. "The eye is the lamp of the body. If your eyes are healthy, your whole body will be full of light. But if your eyes are unhealthy, your whole body will be full of darkness. If then the light within you is darkness, how great is that darkness!" (Matt. 6:22-23 NIV). By careful consideration of what you watch on television, what you look at in the magazines and on the Internet, you decide whether to live a healthy life as a Christian or one that is dark. Any level of darkness can be pretty tricky. You might not see anything wrong with lusting after a man that you see plastered on the front of a magazine or watching an episode of a raunchy drama, but those instances can quickly take over your mind. Our eyes need to be protected because they are the windows to our souls and our hearts. "For as he thinketh in his heart, so is he" (Prov. 23:7). If we don't shield our eyes from sin, our spiritual vision will become blurry, cloudy and eventually completely blinded to the tricks of Satan. Ask God for healthy spiritual vision and go to Him for regular check-ups to catch any early signs of problems that may cause you and the people around you severe damage.

Cheek Color

The next step is all about blush, rouge, cheek color or whatever you like to call it. It can add subtle color to your face and give more definition to your bone structure, especially the cheekbones. Cheek color is available in powder and cream form.

> **TIP:** Use your favorite lip color as a cream blush. Coordinating colors is a breeze when you do this and it's a money and time saver.

Cheek color adds just a little something extra to your face just as God's presence in your life adds a little something extra in your spirit and the things that you do daily. So from now on when you are applying your makeup, especially when you get to the cheek color, acknowledge God and seek Him to give you the lift that you need for the day. I guarantee you He will show up and show out every time. You might start to like cheek color more than you thought you would when you look at it this way. However, just apply it lightly but go all out when you're praising God.

Lip Color

Often times as Christian women we don't want to think of our lips as being beautiful and kissable, but why not? Christian women strive daily to be virtuous and therefore we are attractive on the inside and the outside. We have the right to buy cosmetics and beautify ourselves just as long as we don't stray from our walk with Christ while doing so. The Bible says, "they are not of the world, even as I am not of the world" (John 17:16). Romans 12:2 takes it even further by saying, "And be not conformed to this world: but be ye transformed by the renewing of your mind, that ye may prove what is that good, and acceptable, and perfect, will of God." Christian women do not have to walk around with crusty, cracked lips. I have a saying "It's not what's on the lips it's what comes out of the mouth" and that's from the Gospel according to Megan but also Proverbs 31:26 says "she openeth her mouth with wisdom; and in her tongue is the law of kindness." It didn't mention anything about lipstick or lip-gloss being "un-virtuous." She was virtuous by what came from her lips.

Lipstick pulls your look together so choosing the right color is key. Sometimes you may have to mix colors or visit a professional makeup artist to find that ideal shade. Lipstick fortunately comes in cream, sheer, gloss, matte and frost to create different looks and finishes. I suggest experimenting with an array of colors and finishes until you achieve the best look.

TIP: Use a lip brush for longer lasting, better-looking lip color. Apply from corner of the mouth inward.

Lip liners are also very important because they define the shape of the lip or have the power to create a shape if necessary. Lip liners come in many colors and serve as a guide for lipstick or lip gloss. Together, lip liners and lipstick (or gloss) work to create a great combination and a new sense of self. When my lipstick or lip gloss is that perfect shade, it just boosts my self-esteem. Maybe it's just me but I walk around in hopes that the color will never fade away.

On a spiritual note, your lips are vital to God because they part to give Him praise, speak encouraging words to a neighbor, sing a soothing song to a frustrated child and so on. Don't act like Satan who was known as the angel of praise but wanted to have God's power. Instead let God use you to encourage and uplift others. Take the time to find the appropriate shade of lip color and while you're doing that think of all the kind words to say to a rude co-worker or a depressed relative or even how to deal with that road rage. Do not behave like the Pharisees who worshipped and prayed in vain. "This people draweth near to me with their mouth, and honoreth me with their lips, but their heart is far from me" (Matt. 15:8). Let the words that come from your lips be genuine, kind and helpful.

Regardless of the kinds of things that are going on in your personal life, do not let it affect your praise or opportunity to minister to someone else. When God allowed Satan to test Job who lost his money, his family and his health, Job continued to lift up the name of God. "My lips shall not speak wickedness, nor my tongue utter deceit" (Job 27:4). Now that's some kind of lip service. How many people could still speak kind words after losing so much? Even after Job's supposedly wise friends encouraged him, which seemed more like discouraging him, he still continued to praise God. "My words shall be the uprightness of my heart: and my lips shall utter knowledge" (Job 33:3). In other words Job knew in his heart that everything that he was going through had a purpose and he refrained from speaking negative through the entire process. In the end, "the Lord blessed the latter end of Job more than the beginning," and he was known throughout the land (Job 42:12).

So you see ladies, your lips can either make you or break you. Just as lipstick pulls together your entire look, the words that come from your lips can affect your entire life. Think about this when you put on that lip color in the morning and throughout the day. You should practice saying kind words to your neighbor or coworkers on a daily basis. Your kindness and ability to speak words of wisdom will increase by the day.

You're all set!

It seems to me that you're ready for your speech at the women's conference. Not only do you look fabulous but you also have spiritual insight on some things that I'm sure you have taken for granted for years. Now when someone asks you who did your makeup or what shade of lip color you're wearing, praise God and use that as an opportunity to minister. The best thing of it all is that when you have God in your life people will be able to see the God in you from a mile away. They won't even be surprised when you tell them all about the One who can give them the ultimate makeover.

Notes

Chapter 3

Beauty Transformation

In a world filled with temptations, distractions, setbacks, and destruction it is not uncommon to come across women of God who have not lived their lives as virtuously as desired. Wrong choices have had long-term effects. Befriending people with opposite pursuits in life have caused stagnation. Poor time management or bad financial planning has led to a life of stress and unhappiness. All these and other factors are very real issues that women face but God never leaves us nor does he forsake us. Whether we are in God's will or out, Jesus is praying for us and being patient with us. "The Lord is not slow in keeping his promise, as some understand slowness. He is patient with you, not wanting anyone to perish, but everyone to come to repentance" (2 Pet. 3:9). When we are having mountaintop experiences, everything seems to be great. We can shop at our leisure, husbands are wonderful, kids are great, co-workers are bearable, church is amazing and life is grand. However, when we are having a valley experience we can't ever seem to find a happy medium. Shopping is on a tight budget, family members are irritating, co-workers are annoying, church is unnecessary and life is depressing. Circumstances change, we change, but our faithful God changes not. "I the LORD do not change" (Mal. 3:6). As a matter of fact in Hebrews 13:8 we discover that "Jesus is the same yesterday and today and forever."

During our trials in the fire (and there will be several, notice "trials" is plural) we learn to lean and depend on God. In fact, once we discover that God has never left our side and that our faith needs to be in Him, a beauty transformation can begin. Isaiah 61:2-3 (NIV) says, "to bestow on them a crown of beauty, instead of ashes, the oil of joy, instead of mourning, and a garment of praise, instead of a spirit of despair. They will be called oaks of righteousness, a planting of the LORD for the display of his splendor." God doesn't want us to walk around wallowing in self-pity; this takes away from the beauty of serving others, from the beauty of drawing men and women to Christ and from the beauty of positive words and actions. We are to be happy and not sad as though we have nothing to smile about. There is something to be admired from the heavens to the earth below if we just take the time to appreciate God's creation.

The fiery trials that we endure can truly burn us on many levels. Bad choices, wrong turns, poor judgment, lack of vision, and evil intentions are just a few fire starters that are ignited by our failure to walk away. In reality, burns do not feel good to the body whether it is first-degree or certainly if it's third- or fourth-degree. I worked for a brief amount of time in a Burn Unit. For you to truly understand what the scripture means when it says beauty instead of ashes, you have to consider the process that a burn victim goes through. In order for a burn to heal, new growth and replacement of the damaged layer of skin has to take place. The healing process can take up to two years in some cases. There are several different ways to treat burn victims including laser surgery, Z-plasty, skin grafting or dermabrasion. One of the most excruciating treatments for burn victims is probably dermabrasion because the area that has been burned has to be scraped or shaved away. Although painful and very risky, this process is sometimes necessary in the steps to regenerating the new skin cells. The dermabrasion process helps to improve the victim's scars and appearance throughout and is a result of the healing process. Of course, the patient is given anesthesia to numb the pain during dermabrasion surgery but the thought of having the skin scraped or shaved away can help you better understand the degree of beauty transformation that a burn victim must undergo.

First-Degree Burns

Consider the burns that fiery trials have left on you and your spirit. Some burns are first-degree where you endure a little bit of pain and a little bit of swelling. It's not so serious and only affects a tiny layer of your ego and your spirituality. You cool the pain with a few sermons and a quick read through your Bible that you had to dust off. You apply some over-the-counter cream of prayer every other day until your burn starts to feel better. You heal on your own without much of a need to share your pain with a spiritual advisor. Within a few days because you have no sign of why you were burned or what caused the burn, you're back to your old self again. In the event that your burn was a little overwhelming, you may decide to seek a little emergency help from your "old" accountability partner that you fell off track with a few months ago when your life became hectic.

Second-Degree Burns

Since you never really learned from or perhaps you forgot about your first-degree burns, you find yourself back in the midst of a fiery trial. You knew better, your mind and spirit told you otherwise, but you chose to do things your way, not once but twice. This time because you were burned pretty badly, there are some visible signs of what transpired. Now you have a nasty metaphorical scar and work days seem way too long because you would rather be home sulking about your burns. Everyone around you who seems to be happy now starts to annoy you, because all you can focus on is your painful scar. You don't bounce back from the second-degree burn as fast as the first-degree. You attend worship service more consistently and you go a step further to purchase the CDs and DVDs from sermons that you hadn't even heard during the weekends that you decided to skip service. You are calling your accountability partner more and more and they are wondering why the sudden change of heart. You know that you need more than what your over-the counter cream prayers can offer because bitterness is starting to set in and you don't want to do any further damage to your burns. You begin to spend more time at the hospital (place of worship) to treat your second-degree burn.

Third-Degree Burns

An intention to hurt someone the way they hurt you backfires; a plan to pay someone back does more bad than good, and a choice to move ahead of God ends up causing you a third-degree burn. You end up destroying yourself, friendships, families and all parties involved. The third-degree burn that you have inflicted is the most serious of all burns. You have to seek counsel from a spiritual advisor or a therapist because your ability to heal properly heavily depends upon it. You lay yourself on the throne every chance you get and there is no place that you won't cry out to God. Your scars are so deep that you have to undergo reconstructive surgery in order to get your life and the lives of others back on track. You've burned yourself so bad that you are often numb from feeling emotion. You are sometimes even numb to hearing from God because you feel so unforgiveable, and so despicable about the choices that you allowed yourself to make. You need God, your accountability partner, and your spiritual advisors now more than ever. In your mind, you are in a place of destruction, a place of damage beyond repair. You experience all types of reactions to your actions while you undergo the healing process. The dermabrasion surgery that you have to receive in order to take away the scars that were left from your burn is painful but necessary to your beauty transformation.

Level with God

God knows all of your pains. He knows about the first-degree burns that you self-medicated and then jumped right back into poor judgment before you could really get to the bottom of why you let yourself get burned. God knows about the second-degree burns and sees your half-hearted efforts to get back on the right track. However, you really don't deal with the real reasons why you like being burned. Lastly, God is there with you as you douse yourself with the gasoline of bad choices and even when you hand the matches right over to Satan. Before you know it, WOOP! You're left with a third- or fourth-degree burn.

All burns are not self-inflicted. Most burns are accidental — you ended up in the wrong place at the wrong time, you made a hasty move, you weren't really paying attention to your surroundings or you underestimated the repercussions of your actions or choices. However, many burns are caused by curiosity — you want to see how far you can go before you get caught up or you want to know what something is really like so you go for it.

Sometimes friends, family, co-workers or whomever will unsuspectingly burn you because of the trust that you place in them. You have to watch out for defective people like you have to watch out for defective products that can cause a burn injury when you least expect it. You also don't want to associate yourself with pyromaniacs — those who enjoy being burned, burning other people and who never ever take the opportunity to heal from their past burn injuries. In addition, you don't want to hang around people that are prone to accidental injury in their own life.

Instead, level with God, someone who never leaves you nor forsakes you no matter what choices you make. He wants to heal your first-degree burn and He certainly wants to heal your second- or third-degree burn. God is the Master Healer, the Jehovah Rapha and He is the Balm in Gilead needed to apply to each and every scar. In Exodus 15:26 Moses reminded the Israelites, "If you will diligently obey the Lord your God, and do what is right in his sight, and pay attention to his commandments, and keep all his statutes, then all the diseases that I brought on the Egyptians I will not bring on you, for I, the Lord, am your healer."

The healing process won't be easy. Remember burn victims sometimes have to wait up to two years for the healing to be complete. Likewise, healing from a serious burn or a series of burns in your life must take time. First-, second- and third-degree burns can be treated and that's when restoration occurs. Therefore, don't allow fiery trials to burn you to the core leaving nothing but ashes, the residue that remains after something burns up completely or decays. For the ancient Israelites, ashes were symbolical for great sadness and mourning. They were very public about showing their period of mourning or to display sadness in their lives. I encourage you instead to trade in your ashes or the remnants of your burns for beauty. Be reminded of the Hebrew boys that went into the fiery furnace but came out without a trace that they had been near a fire. "All the important people, the government leaders and king's counselors, gathered around to examine them and discovered that the fire hadn't so much as touched the three men — not a hair singed, not a scorch mark on their clothes, not even the smell of fire on them!" (Daniel 3:27). Allow God to bring you out looking and smelling brand new. If you have or are currently undergoing reconstructive surgery, let go and let God. Endure the pain, embrace the process, and empower those around you when you have been delivered.

35

Notes

Chapter 4

A Natural Look

Imagine your delight when a package that you've been waiting on from FedEx or UPS has arrived. The person on the other end of the spectrum is also relieved that their valuables have been retrieved by its rightful owner. Everyone involved is happy and the priceless package has been successfully delivered. Similar events occur in the atmosphere when we are successfully delivered from our fiery trials and tribulations. God is a proud Father looking down from His throne of mercy and grace, our family and friends are elated and we are now driven with so much purpose that it would take an army to throw us off our path. However, in all honesty it's not impossible to be distracted by tricks, trials and tribulations for Satan is always seeking whom he can devour 24 hours a day, 7 days a week, 365 days out of the year because "we wrestle not against flesh and blood, but against principalities, against powers, against the rulers of the darkness of this world, against spiritual wickedness in high places" (Eph. 6:12). With this piece of information that Paul shares in this verse, we've got to always be on guard. We have to make sure we are planted in a flourishing place of worship and we have to surround ourselves with people that can and will hold us accountable for our actions. Most importantly, we have to make good use of our time. In other words, when we are delivered from sickness, dangerous relationships, a stressful job, damaging friendships, financial burdens or whatever, it is vital that we are consistent in giving God our talents, our tissue and most importantly our time.

Remaining Faithful

You've gotten the breakthrough that you wanted and now you can exhale just a little bit. Your prayers were answered and your storm is now over! You can relax and catch up on the latest news with your co-workers on your lunch break. Right? Not so fast. How long will you remain faithful as a prayer warrior, serving at church, testifying everywhere you go and do so just as diligently as you did when you were in need of God's mercy and grace? After the waves of life that have thrown us and jolted us have calmed down, we tend to turn away from the same God that kept us in the midst of our storm. Why is this? Mainly because we get complacent and think that we have arrived. Another reason may be that we often feel so beat up and shipwrecked after our storm that we just want to be "normal" again. After a while, we begin making excuses about how busy we are on the same job that we asked God for and received. We use the same gifts that God gave us in every other capacity BUT to build up the Kingdom. We fail to give to God and others with the very same provisions that God has bestowed upon us. *We* begin to be our biggest problems.

Sometimes being "normal" or being in a relaxed mode can mean being distracted by things that separate us from our number one love. No matter what, we must remain faithful in doing the things that keep us connected to God. According to the American Heritage Illustrated Encyclopedic Dictionary, *remain* means "to continue in a specified condition, quality or place; to endure or persist." Therefore, the faith that you had when you were trusting God to deliver you should still be strong and present even after your storm has been removed. You've heard the saying, "You're either in a storm, headed to a storm, or on your way out of a storm." That is a sheer indicator that remaining faithful in praying, serving and inspiring others is absolutely necessary all the time! 1 Thessalonians 5:17 says, "Pray without ceasing." Remain faithful by praying for the storm you're in and the storm you'll be in next week, next month or next year. Serve at your church and in your community whether your storm is over or not. Remain faithful to serving other people because your testimony can impact someone else's life or their testimony will inspire you. Instead of always joining your co-workers for lunch or watching TV for hours on end after work, study God's word, sing hymns of praise and continue doing those things that strengthen your relationship with The One who loves you most; The One who always remains faithful to you. "God is faithful (reliable, trustworthy, and therefore ever true to His promise, and He can be depended on)..." (1 Cor. 1:9 AMP).

A Time For Everything

Have you ever bumped into a friend or old co-worker at a grocery store or post office and you decide to connect again after five or so years only to find out that you've evolved and they haven't? They are still partying every weekend when you simply go out every blue moon or on a special occasion. Their language reminds you of the language that you used when you were in high school but now you're a parent so you've toned it down, to say the least. The list goes on and on but the bottom line is you realize how much you've grown and how others around you have become stagnant in their growth for various reasons. Be mindful that it happens and we have to love people where they are and pray for growth in the areas where they need it most. In life however, certain choices lead to definite outcomes and there's a time to grow up.

You're in for a rude awakening if you're still wishing for the days when you could hang out until the wee hours of the morning, or when you were single without a husband and kids, or when your toughest decision was whether you wanted to supersize your fries. The truth is the times that you may sit and long for, have come and gone and you have to accept your current season. If you remain stuck in the past, how can God elevate you in the now?

Remember there is a time for everything. There is a time to be single and there is a time to be married. There is a time to have no responsibilities and there is a time to own up to your responsibilities. There is a time to be self-full and there is a time to be self-less. There is a time to hang out with associates and there is a time to let go of people who don't support you or hold you accountable. You have to make the best decisions for your life.

I'm reminded of a song by Rev. Milton Brunson titled "For the Good of Them". The lyrics are, "the race is not given to the swift, nor to the strong. But to the one that endures until the end. There will be problems and sometimes you'll walk alone, but I know that

I know that I know, things will work out, yes they will. For the good of them who love the Lord." You've got to endure until the end even if that means making major changes in your life. Everything will work itself out in the end especially if you are keeping your eyes on the things of God and building His Kingdom.

Making Good Use of Your Time

At some point you have to discover God's purpose for your life, accept that purpose and start walking in that purpose. If you don't know what your purpose is, let's stop right now and pray.

Dear God,

Help me to discover my purpose. It is that gift that has been stirring up in me and that comes to me naturally. It is that treasure that has been staring me in my face for years that I have yet to accept. It is the beautiful seed that you planted in me when I was being formed in my mother's womb. Use me, God. I know what I have a passion to do and what you have entrusted me to do while on this earth. Help me to accept the gift(s) that you have placed inside of me and to move forward in your will for my life. Plant me in a thriving church with a pastor who will help lead me into my destiny, surround me with Godly people who will encourage me every step of the way and give me a heart to serve others all the days of my life. I ask these things in your darling Son Jesus' name. Amen.

Notes

Chapter 5

Covering It Up

Kami lay in bed looking at the ceiling contemplating on whether she should even bother to go to work in the morning. On the other side of town, Jeri is studying her Bible before she decides to call it a night. Terry is having the time of her life at the hot, new dance club celebrating its grand opening. Nicholette is checking her email one last time, chatting on instant messenger and updating her Facebook status yet again. What do all these women have in common? They all have sinned and fallen short of God's glory in the past week. It doesn't matter who did what, how often or how likely they are to fall into the same trap again, "for all have sinned and fallen short of the glory of God" (Rom. 3:23). God does however expect us to put forth an effort to live holy and strive to set ourselves apart.

God doesn't measure sin by categories like we tend to do. We tend to measure murder and adultery on different levels from lying or gossiping. Whatever the case or whatever the sin, God loves us just the same. We can't understand God's rationale of how He can take an ex-stripper and turn her into a renowned speaker. Or how a former drug addict can now have a non-profit organization that helps current drug abusers find a new way of life. We can't figure out how even though we have lived our own lives in such a reckless manner that God still has a purpose for us. These miraculous events sometimes go beyond our scope of thinking but God's "thoughts are not [our] thoughts, neither are [His] ways [our] ways" (Isa. 55:8).

The list can go on and on of how God can deliver a person from a life of sin, and yes, He can deliver you!

Concealer

In the world of makeup, concealer is used to cover up blemishes, dark circles, redness and acne scars. Concealer gives the appearance of flawless skin. Some women are fortunate enough to have blemish free skin but many women are grateful to concealer for its ability to cover their imperfections even if it's only for a few hours. Applying concealer is a unique process within itself. After choosing the right color to apply, concealer works best when it is lightly tapped onto the surface of the skin. This gentle application blends the concealer into the skin more evenly. It reminds me of the gentle taps of mercy and grace that God applies in our lives to get us through those dark situations that have the potential to leave scars on us or others. Once the concealer is applied to all the blemishes on the skin, then foundation and the other steps to makeup can continue. If time isn't taken to cover blemishes with concealer, the additional steps that a woman takes to apply her makeup can be pointless. The makeup will still look nice; it just won't be as excellent as it could've been. Any makeup artist would agree.

On a spiritual note, when we take the time to confess our sins to God and possibly to another trusted person, then God will cover our sins just as concealer does. It will allow you to move forward in life not just in good standing but in excellent standing. You won't have to look in the mirror wishing you had taken the time to cover up the blemishes that you now see. You will be able to face yourself and know that you paced yourself, took time to devote to self and the beauty of your transformation will be visible.

The Finished Product

Most women who have to wear an abundance of concealer on a daily basis still search for ways to improve the surface of their skin from blemishes, scars and dark spots. That desire to look as best as possible and hopefully improving skin for the better is a very natural thing to do. The woman on a constant search for something better has an innate drive to improve the finished product — the look of her skin with or without makeup.

In essence, God sees us as the finished product. He appreciates when we put in the work that is required to be better in our many roles as women. However, God doesn't see us with the mistakes that we've made or the times that we chose the opposite of His best for our lives. When our choices in life have taken us outside of God's will, He still sees us for what He made us to be. Once we align ourselves with God, He can then move us into our destiny. It's not an overnight process. Like with any product a woman buys to improve the look of her skin, it takes several weeks before there are any noticeable changes. The same type of patience, understanding and trust is needed with God. Depending on the amount of blemishes and the deepness of our scars it will take some time for noticeable changes to occur. You might be thinking, "Well if God is the same yesterday, today and forever more, then why doesn't He immediately change my situation?" It's a two-way street. Remember I stated earlier that we have to be PATIENT, UNDERSTANDING and TRUST that God will move on our behalf. If we get impatient and start looking at the situations in our lives with our natural eye as opposed to our spiritual eye then we are bound to throw in the towel right on the verge of our breakthrough.

Forgiveness

There is a process to being patient, being understanding and placing our trust in people and also our Lord and Savior. We tend to look at life differently when people that we have depended on to take care of us and be there for us turn their backs or hurt us beyond repair. We take matters into our own hands when God seems to ignore our cries or doesn't seem to answer our prayers in our time. The culprit that can take us further than we want to go, keep us longer than we want to stay, and make us say things and act like we don't know right from wrong is UNFORGIVENESS. Walking around holding grudges and keeping up walls is not only unhealthy but it's also a dangerous weed in the garden of growth.

Hang in there. Know that God wants to use you and Satan wants to keep you from understanding how valuable you are. God has forgiven you; your sins are covered like concealer covers a blemish. Your sins are no more, no matter who tries to remind you of them or how a situation may look, you are forgiven. Don't waver; fight for yourself and for the people whose lives you are supposed to touch. If you give up and give in then you will be letting Satan win and God's

Kingdom will suffer. God has not brought you this far to leave you. You are His beloved daughter. You are royalty.

Facing Fear

There is nothing that can hold you back from operating in your purpose more so than fear. Unforgiveness and fear are like cousins that come from the same family of weakness and demonic strongholds. Once you have conquered forgiveness of yourself and others, the next big challenge is to combat fear. You may begin to fear whether your past will hold you back or if people will believe that you are all of a sudden ready to walk in your purpose. Before you know it, fear will swallow you and your dreams up and cause you to stand in the same spot for weeks, months, or years. Now you may better understand Franklin D. Roosevelt's famous quote, "There's nothing to fear but fear itself." Fear is debilitating, will steal your dreams and bring your purpose to an end faster than it begins.

The Merriam-Webster's Collegiate Dictionary defines fear as "an unpleasant often strong <u>emotion</u> caused by <u>anticipation</u> or awareness of danger." In other words, fear comes from the expectation that something will go wrong or that someone will cause you harm. Even though we live in a world filled with unseen dangers, God never puts his children in harm's way. Therefore, the notion of fear or anticipation of a problem is not of God. You've heard the saying that "fear is false evidence appearing real" and when you think about it the concept rings true. When I was much younger I was deathly afraid of cockroaches and water bugs because in my mind if

I attempted to kill one, it would grow in size and overpower me with its tentacles. I know that it sounds ridiculous (and gross) but that's just how afraid I was of an average sized bug. If I saw a cockroach I'd scream for my daddy, run in the opposite direction, and trust that my daddy would take care of the bug. Although I hate that my example of fear involves a critter, my response of relying on my daddy can be paralleled to relying on our Daddy in heaven to take care of our problems when we feel we are incapable. I knew that my earthly father would come and get rid of the bug that I feared most and put me at ease until the next incident. On that same note, we have to rely on our Heavenly Father to come and rescue us and fight our battles of fear for us. "The Lord will fight for you; you need only to be still" (Exod. 14:14 NIV). No matter what you fear, with God you can rise above it.

For so long I thought that I needed to go on the Maury Povich talk show to get over my fear of a certain critter but instead another incident helped me to conquer my fear. When I became a mother my desire to protect my most prized possession, my daughter, overruled any degree of fear. If any critter came in close proximity of my daughter it was as if a supernatural power would come over me and I'd kill a critter with my bare hands if necessary. After it was all over I'd cringe at the thought that I even had the strength to kill a bug but it was then that I realized that I was no longer a slave to fear in that arena.

Our fears don't need to be sorted out by a hypnotist on a nationally televised talk show. We have to protect our dreams and purposes with a supernatural power that is given to us by God. 2 Timothy 1:7 reminds us that "God has not given us the spirit of fear; but of power, and of love, and of a sound mind." We have to operate out of boldness and grab what we fear most with our bare hands and crush its very existence. You are a victorious warrior and by faith "the righteous are bold as a lion" (Prov. 28:1). At the onset of fear, remember the Joshua 1:9 (NIV) plea for you to "be strong and courageous. Do not be afraid; do not be discouraged, for the LORD your God will be with you wherever you go." So put your mind at ease and allow God to lead the way to a purpose-filled and fearless life.

Notes

Chapter 6

Taking It All Off

At the end of the day, no matter how tired you are, if you wear makeup you have to take the time to remove it and cleanse your skin. You could choose not to but you'd be dealing with a mess the next morning. Once you remove every trace of makeup, your skin is in its natural state and spiritually this represents who you really are. Wearing makeup does not mean that you're trying to cover up the real you, but there's nothing wrong with admiring who you are without all the makeup. Even if you have acne, blemishes, and scars and you're in the process of fixing your skin problems, when you are au naturale this is how God sees you. We can always find problems with ourselves and be overly critical of ourselves in one way or the other. However, God created you and in His eyes you are "fearfully and wonderfully made" (Ps. 139:14). This doesn't mean that you shouldn't indulge in beauty treatments and skin care regimens, it just means that you should always accept who you really are underneath it all. Remain pleased with yourself from head to toe, inside and outside, on your way to where you're going.

Know Your Worth

Do you know how valuable you are? Do you know how much you are worth? Proverbs 31:10 (NIV) says that a "wife of noble character" is "worth far more than rubies." I figure that this applies not only to a wife but any woman of noble character. What does it mean to be noble? It's someone who is righteous, good or gracious. Do any of those words describe you? Why? Why not? What about character, what does that mean? It's someone with integrity, someone who is honest, strong, determined, and reliable. Do any of those qualities describe you? Why? Why not?

Let's focus for a minute on the statement that describes a wife of noble character as one that is "worth far more than rubies" (Proverbs 31:10 NIV). How valuable are rubies exactly? We often hear that diamonds are a woman's best friend but this verse seems to highlight rubies as being pretty valuable. Rubies were and still are very valuable because they are the "rarest and most precious of all jewels. Thus, they serve in the Bible as an appropriate standard for comparing other things that are even more precious (wisdom, knowledge, a good wife, etc.)" (Nelson, 1995). Rubies are just as valuable as diamonds and only rank second to diamonds in hardness and its fine quality. What's more, "fine-quality rubies are among the costliest of all gems" (World Book, 1996). Rubies are made all over the world in places like Burma, Thailand and India. Although India's rubies have been known to be of lesser quality, India produces the star rubies that are of excellent quality. This thought is an indication that certain circumstances, people, places, associations, etc. can have an effect on the quality of a person. Even when someone comes from a less than ideal situation they can still turn out to be a star ruby.

Millions of fake rubies are manufactured each year to provide a more inexpensive stone to consumers. "However, a demand for real gems has allowed the natural stones to maintain their high value" (World Book, 1996). Although some experts find it hard to distinguish the synthetic stones from the natural stones, there just isn't a substitute for the real thing.

The need for realness will always make women of virtue highly valuable. It may seem as though women of standard, class, dignity, etc. are not as desirable but that is the furthest thing from the truth. On the same note, it may seem that women who devalue themselves by dressing scantily clad, or women who use their bodies and their outer beauty to bring up their value can pass as real but there is no substitute for the real class and virtue of a Godly woman.

Acceptance

The fact that there are so many types of rubies is an indication that on this earth exists all types of women from all walks of life. Some of you reading this book have been divorced, are single mothers, have had abortions, have been raped, have been promiscuous, have abused alcohol, have indulged in homosexuality, bi-sexuality, and even the lifestyle of swinging. The list can go on and on of things that you've done in the past that you aren't necessarily proud of or have caught grief from other people about. No matter where you've been and what you've done, God still accepts you and wants what's best for you. It is still your job to fulfill the purpose that God has called upon you to do. You need to know that you are still worth far more than rubies and that you are still valuable to the body of Christ. Don't allow Satan to steal your vision and your destiny. John 10:10 says, "the thief comes only to steal and kill and destroy" and this is what Satan does all day long. He puts people and situations in your life to throw you off your path of fulfilling your purpose. In Job 1:7 (NIV), "The Lord said to Satan, 'Where have you come from?' Satan answered the Lord, 'From roaming throughout the earth, going back and forth on it.'" That tells you that Satan takes his job of stealing, killing, and destroying you very serious. He spends his days going back and forth, around and around, to create traps for men and women of God. If you fail to accept that you are royalty and that you are valuable beyond your flaws, then you will fall right into Satan's many traps. Accept today that you are "fearfully and wonderfully made" (Ps. 139:14) and that your past does not dictate your future.

Woman In The Mirror

Now that you realize that you are valuable and you accept that you have a great future, it's time to take a look in the mirror. Believe it or not some women can't take a real look at themselves in the mirror. I don't mean looking in the mirror to check to see if your hair is out of place or if your lipstick needs reapplying. I mean a real, long hard look at you. You might be thinking, "Yes, I can look at myself in the mirror!" Okay well do it right now! Go into your bathroom or bedroom and look in the mirror or use your pocket mirror. Complete the Woman in the Mirror activity in the Self-Discovery section of this book starting on page 115.

I hope after completing the activity, you have gained some insight on how you view yourself and how others view you as well.

No matter what you've been told or think of yourself, you are a beautiful, intelligent, influential, and successful woman of God. Everyone who crosses your path will be able to glean from your life's experience and your positive outlook on the future. God allowed you to go through your trials and tribulations and was patient with you when you went left instead of right so in the end He could get all the glory.

Self-Esteem

We learn about self-esteem probably somewhere around middle or junior high school. By the time we get into adulthood we seem to forget the principle of having high self-esteem. Instead we let people walk all over us and dictate to us what is right and what is wrong. We follow the wrong crowd of people in order to fit in. We make poor choices to be a part of the group. By the time we finish being influenced by other people who personally have no morals, standards or boundaries, we are left broken, bruised and used.

Self-esteem is defined as having self-respect, a feeling of pride for oneself, and having confidence and ultimate satisfaction in the way that you feel about yourself. You can either have low self-esteem or high self-esteem. If you have high self-esteem then you exhibit an abundance of respect for yourself and you are satisfied with who you are, how you are and where you are. On the other hand, someone with low self-esteem has a very low level of respect for themselves, lacks confidence and is not satisfied with themselves in some shape, form or fashion.

The way you think about yourself physically, mentally, and emotionally defines your self-esteem. People are often unaware of their individual levels of self-esteem and how it affects their actions in everyday situations. People who have high levels of self-esteem are eager to try new things and tend to do things to their heart's content. Those with low self-esteem often shy away from opportunities or will let people treat them any kind of way. Problems arise when we compare ourselves to others as well as what we constantly see on television, in magazines, and so forth. People come in all shapes, sizes and colors and no one is better than the other. Our society has defined beauty, fashion, music, religion and many other factors to be a certain way and anything else is ugly, not stylish or just plain wrong. The key is to define your own style and attitude, while taking only a few tips from magazines, television or the people you observe on a daily basis.

Go ahead and take the self-esteem quiz on page 124 to see where you rank. It's important that you know how you feel about yourself, the talents that you possess and where you see yourself in your future. The knowledge of your self-esteem level will also give you an idea of what you need to work on and exactly how you need to improve. Hurry back!

Now that you know your ranking you have a job to do. If you have high self-esteem, your job is to keep up the great work and influence others to greatness. If you're in between or you have a low level of self-esteem, your job is to stay focused, strive for greatness, surround yourself with positive people, and keep reading positive books and articles. Glenn Schiraldi has written several books that deal with self-esteem, two of which are entitled *Building Self-Esteem: A 125 Day Program* and *The Self-Esteem Workbook*. You can also visit The National Association for Self-Esteem at www.self-esteem-nase. org or contact your local library or YMCA for assistance in finding a local group that focuses on building self-esteem. Low self-esteem can and will lead to serious cases of depression. If you suffer from seriously low self-esteem or know of someone who does, be sure to talk to a pastor, counselor, family member, friend or accountability partner.

Confidence

How you carry yourself is how others perceive you. Unemployment could be your current occupation, a grandparent could be on their death bed and your house could be days away from foreclosure. However, everything will be okay if you exude confidence no matter what. On the same note if you walk around with little or no confidence people will perceive you to be weak, a complainer, a quitter, a lazy person or even worse. Psalm 71:5 (NIV) says, "For you have been my hope, Sovereign LORD, my confidence since my youth." Therefore, go back to the confidence that you had when you were young. The attitude that you could do anything! The confidence that you would ace your spelling test or that you would blow your teacher away with your science project. The confidence that you had when you told the new girl at school not to flirt with *your* boyfriend or the confidence that you had when

57

you told your parents what your plans would be after high school. There was a time in your youth that you were unstoppable, when you had the world on your shoulders and you dared anyone to move it. That same confidence is in you because God put it there for the purpose that He has for your life. You've just got to rediscover the confident person that you were created to be.

Rediscovering Your Confidence

Tell yourself these words:

> *God created a confident woman in me. I am free of doubt. I am self-assured. I am aware of myself, my powers and my abilities. I am all of these things because God created me this way and God makes no mistakes. I know that my hope rests in the Lord on those days when I don't feel so confident because God will lift me back up where I belong. I exude confidence no matter what my circumstance. I am determined to walk out that door with a smile on my face, because of His grace, I can maintain.*

Say this expression of confidence as much as you need to and especially on those days when you are under attack. Just the very act of speaking this into existence will remind you of your worth, your confidence and what God said He would do on your behalf. "For the LORD will be your confidence and will keep your foot from being taken" (Prov. 3:26).

It's very important to understand that confidence is a by-product of faith. If you have faith that God's word is true, that He will do what He said He would do and that you can live a life of peace, no worries or doubt, and experience joy as a child of God then you will walk around with sheer confidence. It seems pretty simple but it's not simple at all. Satan wants to diminish your faith and shatter your confidence and either you will let him win or you will fight for what is rightfully yours. You deserve to live in peace, you deserve a life that's worry-free, and you deserve to have confidence exude from you.

Beauty of Strength

Your beauty lies in your strength. Therefore, anything that takes away from your strength or takes you away from staying strong has to be put in its place. In other words, neglecting your body by not eating right, failing to exercise regularly, or not getting proper rest has to be dealt with accordingly. In addition, distractions like bringing work home from your job, wasting time on the phone gossiping, spending too much time on social networks and not enough time on you can cause major problems. You have to be strong spiritually, mentally, physically, emotionally, and not to mention financially.

Strength of Being A Mother

The role of a mother is one that is such a beautiful privilege. You carry a child in your womb for ten months and you anticipate the moment when you will see the face of your prince or princess. You bond with your child long before he/she arrives and your voice is familiar to them before they lay eyes on you or lay their heads on your chest. Your heartbeat is a familiar sound that lulls your baby to sleep and is what your bundle of joy was accustomed to for months.

When scared, frustrated, hungry or sleepy, one thing your baby can depend on is you. You come packaged with that familiar voice, heartbeat and a strength that is recognized for the first time and one that your child will emulate for the rest of their life.

The strength that you possess as a mother comes from the choices that you make from beginning to end: choosing to become a mother, to eat healthy, live healthy and protect your unborn child from any hurt or danger. Your strength comes from wanting the best for your child and sacrificing to make sure that your child has every opportunity to be successful. Your strength comes from your strong desire to raise up a woman or man of God. Your strength comes from reading to your child, making rules for your child and shaping your child for a bright future. If you have yet to become a mother, you may have decided that the time wasn't right or you may have unfortunately lost your child. However, you too possess a strength of determination to one day be a great mother.

Strength of Being a Wife

Marriage is a ministry. Therefore you should conduct yourself within a marriage as you would if you were a part of a ministry. You wouldn't try to run everything, you wouldn't show up late to every meeting or event, you wouldn't snap at your ministry leader or give him the silent treatment. You wouldn't storm out of the room when you couldn't have your way. You wouldn't call your ministry leader's mother to ask her how could she raise such a selfish ministry leader and you certainly wouldn't pray and ask God to deliver you from your ministry. Sounds funny but this is how women should think of marriage. Your role as a wife is a privilege and your strength is one that is admired by many.

As a wife, your strength lies in being supportive and understanding your role. Your role is not to be the leader of your husband but to help and be a disciplinarian to your children. Together you and your husband seek God on every issue no matter how minute or magnanimous. Your strength comes from waiting on your husband to apply what God says to do next. Your strength comes in equipping your children with what they need to do when God speaks to and through your husband. In the event that God reveals a message to you, your strength comes in relaying the message to your husband and waiting on him to decide how the family will move.

Strength of Being A Sister

My sister and I talk on the phone so much that I'm afraid one of these days our service provider will join our conversation to ask if we have any other people that we could talk to besides each other. Real sisters are inseparable. Whether you are connected to your sister by blood or by life's circumstances the value of your relationship is priceless. Friends come and go but a sister stays by your side no matter what. A real sister is not jealous, competitive, fake or two-faced. A real sister lifts you up when you are down, celebrates with you and motivates you beyond what you can see for yourself. A real sister sees what you can't see, hears what you can't hear and shares her mistakes so you won't make the same. A real sister is irreplaceable because she is heaven sent, genuine and amazing. Your sister may not have the finest clothes, cars or other material things but she has wisdom that is far more valuable. Your sister may not have attained the highest degree or any degree at all but her level of education is not determined by man. Your sister may have never traveled across the country but her paths in life have afforded her a wealth of knowledge and common sense. Your sister may not speak eloquently or use big words, but when she speaks you listen because her words always soothe your soul better than any prolific speaker. Your sister was made by God specifically for you. God knew what you would need in your sister before you knew; God knew all the trials and tribulations that you and your sister both would endure in life so that you could miraculously be there for one another.

Don't ever discount your sister. Friends are in our lives for a reason, a season and if you're fortunate a lifetime but a sister is there for an eternity. If you have a broken relationship with a sister, work to mend it. If your sister doesn't live the way you want her to live, be more understanding and figure out how to be in each other's lives. Remember God knows what path we will take in life before we take it. If your sister lives in a different state than you, visit more often or pick one day out of the week dedicated to catching up on the latest news, praying for one another and providing encouragement and counsel. If your sister is incarcerated, visit her often and even figure out a way that you can minister to your sister and the other ladies as well. If your sister is deceased, commemorate her by developing a ministry or non-profit organization in her name, or develop a scholarship fund to help neighborhood children who would go to school to major in your late sister's field. If your sister is lost and unsaved, pray mightily for her life. If she has run away from home and you know where she is whether it's in the streets, the homeless shelter or the crack house, go pray with her, take her a Bible and a different book (like this one) and once a month take her a new book or material to read. Speak life over her dead situation, ask God to revive your sister and demand her back from the pits of hell.

Strength of Being A True Friend

A friend is like a sister but in most cases not born of the same parents. A true friend seems like you were separated at birth and no one bothered to tell you. When you hurt, a true friend hurts. When you celebrate, a true friend brings the balloons and confetti. A true friend loves you when you're up and encourages you when you are down. A true friend knows when to talk and when to just sit quietly and listen. A true friend pushes you to go beyond your comfort zone and doesn't complain when you expect the same.

A great example of friendship was displayed in a biblical reference by Solomon in Proverbs 18:24 about Jesus, "...a friend sticks closer than a brother." For the sake of this situation, we can change "brother" to "sister." Just like sisters, true friends will have disagreements, conflicts and will need periods of space for growth and self-evaluation. Times like these don't indicate dysfunction in the relationship; it only means that there is always room for improvement even in the best friendships. The true test comes when trials and tribulations arise and nothing will separate the two.

Strength of Being An Accountability Partner

In life there will come a time (or two or three) when you will need to lean on someone for help. You will be in dire need of some sound advice and wise counsel. As you go through life you will begin to realize that everyone is not qualified to give you the advice that you need when you are making a life-changing decision. You may visit your pastor from time to time, or go to therapy/counseling sessions once a month but what do you do in the meantime? You eventually connect yourself to an accountability partner who may be a close friend, relative or church member. No matter where you met your accountability partner their role in your life is of extreme importance. Your role as an accountability partner is also valuable.

Strength of Being You

You were born exactly the way God envisioned you. No matter how tall or short, fat or skinny, rich or poor, God knew exactly what he had in store for you and your life. "Before I formed you in the womb I knew you, before you were born I set you apart; I appointed you as a prophet to the nations" (Jer. 1:5 NIV). Therefore, hold your head up high, stick your chest out and fight on through whatever battle you're facing in life. God has not forgotten you no matter how things appear or how you may feel at this very moment. When you can't trace Him, you've got to trust Him and the strength of being you is knowing that God has your back, your front and sides too.

You were created in God's image, and you are so important to God in every way. The proof is in His word:

> *"Are not two little sparrows sold for a penny? And yet not one of them will fall to the ground without your Father's leave (consent) and notice. But even the very hairs of your head are all numbered. Fear not, then; you are of more value than many sparrows"(Matt. 10:29-31 AMP).*

If Satan can keep you from knowing how valuable you are then he has won generations of battles. You were placed on this earth for a purpose and to touch lives in your community and across the nation. Your legacy is meant to live on through generations and if you refuse to take your position starting today, then you can and will be replaced. God's perfect will on this earth must be carried forth just as it is in heaven; His will is going to come forth with or without you. Take every opportunity to be used by God, accept the calling that's on your life and get busy. It's not written anywhere that it will be an easy road but you must get busy building God's kingdom. When you recognize the strength of being you and begin walking in your purpose (or you've been walking in your purpose for a while), don't expect a lot of people to be on the same road to righteousness or to even understand why you are so passionate about God's Great Commission. Matthew 9:37 informs us that "the harvest is plentiful, but the workers are few." This was the case in biblical times and such will be the case until Christ returns. In addition, if you are looking for applause and easy reception from everyone you share Christ's message with, know that this may not always come right away or at all. When you feel your strength wavering from the weariness of the battle remember Psalm 121:

> *"I will lift up mine eyes unto the hills, from whence cometh my help. My help cometh from the LORD, which made heaven and earth. He will not suffer thy foot to be moved: he that keepeth thee will not slumber. Behold, he that keepeth Israel shall neither slumber nor sleep. The LORD is thy keeper: the LORD is thy shade upon thy right hand. The sun shall not smite thee by day, nor the moon by night. The LORD shall preserve thee from all evil: he shall preserve thy soul. The LORD shall preserve thy going out and thy coming in from this time forth, and even for evermore."*

You always have the strength of God to lean and depend on. God will be waiting when you're ready to make your step. He will not force you to do anything because He deals with us on a free will basis. However, I refuse to function in this life without God's provision, protection and prosperity and I wouldn't advise you to do the same. Recognize your strength and who you have in your corner. "Do not be afraid of them; the Lord your God himself will fight for you" (Deut. 3:22 NIV). You can't lose!

Chapter 7

What Is The Big Secret?

If you've ever had a secret to tell or someone told you a secret, you know the thrill and excitement that it brings. Not the kind of secret that involves something negative about someone but the kind of secret that may be to surprise someone or a plan to do or say something that will change someone's life forever. This is how I feel about my experience of going on a sabbatical five years ago. My life was changed so dramatically and I want to share the secret of my evolution with you. I want to clue you in on the secret that needs to be told — the fulfillment of a sabbatical.

Sabbatical Defined

In biblical days, a sabbatical was observed every seventh year under the Mosaic Law, during which time the land was given rest, debts were forgiven, etc.

> *"For six years you are to sow your fields and harvest the crops, but during the seventh year let the land lie unplowed and unused. Then the poor among your people may get food from it, and the wild animals may eat what is left. Do the same with your vineyard and your olive grove" (Exod. 23:10-11 NIV).*

The spirit of generosity was heavily encouraged during the sabbatical year and freedom was granted to those that had been enslaved. As one would expect, there was a proper protocol on how the canceling of debts were to be done:

> *"At the end of every seven years you must cancel debts. This is how it is to be done: Every creditor shall cancel any loan they have made to a fellow Israelite. They shall not require payment from anyone among their own people, because the LORD's time for canceling debts has been proclaimed. You may require payment from a foreigner, but you must cancel any debt your fellow Israelite owes you" (Deut. 15:1-3 NIV).*

There was a sense of renewal that took place in the land and in people's lives. Could you imagine being a slave and you wake up one morning to find out that you and your family are free? What if all the money you owed to credit card companies and other outstanding debt would all be erased? You'd probably wonder if there was a catch or you'd think that it was too good to be true. Well when God says it, that settles it! Even for those who had to free the slaves and cancel debt owed to them by others, the act of obedience to God was far more than what they would've received:

> *"...there need be no poor people among you, for in the land the LORD your God is giving you to possess as your inheritance, he will richly bless you, if only you fully obey the LORD your God and are careful to follow all these commands I am giving you today. For the LORD your God will bless you as he has promised, and you will lend to many nations but will borrow from none. You will rule over many nations but none will rule over you." (Deut. 15:4-6 NIV)*

It was a win-win situation for both parties involved and the same applies to people in our day in time who decide to participate in modern-day sabbaticals in some shape, form or fashion.

A sabbatical is very similar to fasting as far as the principle of sacrificing something to get closer to God. However, the difference is that a sabbatical doesn't necessarily involve giving up food or only consuming juice and water for a period of time. A sabbatical is more or less changing your normal routine for a period of time; it's a period of rest from your usual daily operations. It is a way to connect with the core of who you are and a time when you can finally find the answers to some of your most puzzling questions about your purpose, where God is leading you and how you can be stretched to your next level. If you are always spiraling out of control with the rigmarole of life — career, family, friends, hobbies, etc., it is hard sometimes to discover what you really want out of life. We often try to plan for marriage, plan for children, plan for a vacation, plan for this and that but you will never really be fully prepared for too much of anything. Instead, it's best to learn how to roll with the punches and keep your head on straight no matter what season you're in. Paul instructed us in Philippians 4:11 (NIV) to "be content whatever the circumstances." In that same verse, Paul stated that he had to learn to be content through any situation; don't miss the major point that some things have to be learned, set aside, and an effort has to be put forth. If all of this describes you, then a sabbatical may be just what you need to get you back on track in life. It may be exactly what you need to propel you forward past the spot you've been stuck in for the past few years.

Any amount of time that you set aside to get closer to God can be defined as a sabbatical. Be sure to determine what you are going to focus on during your alone time with God.

My Personal Experience

After having my daughter out of wedlock, the family counselor, Dr. Earnest Mottley, instructed me to go on a sabbatical. He felt that I needed to take one year to get back where I needed to be with my relationship with God. I had heard of a sabbatical when you take a Sunday off after a weeklong revival or Vacation Bible School but nothing like this. Dr. Mottley indicated that I didn't need any distractions such as dating, unnecessary socializing, etc. Agreeing to the sabbatical that he suggested would mean that for 365 days I'd be giving up anything that would keep me from getting closer to God and developing a strong relationship with my daughter. It seemed like a daunting task at the onset; I certainly wondered how I could go an entire year without dating anyone but the question really was how could I not? Even the thought of missing out on dating or the social scene was a sheer indication that my priorities were not in order.

About six months into my sabbatical and after reading a book that Dr. Mottley suggested called *Choosing God's Best* by Dr. Dan Raunikar, God began to stir up the gifts that were inside of me. It was during that time that I began writing this book. I also intensely studied the Bible, another instruction by Dr. Mottley. During my sabbatical, my sensitivity to God's Word was on a level that I had never experienced. Scriptures that I'd normally look over or read too fast without getting a Word from God would stand out in ways like never before. My closeness to God created a hunger in me to know more about God, not just His will for my life, but I craved to know more about a God who loved me even when I ignored Him.

I became enthralled by the Book of Esther because I realized that Esther and I had a lot in common. We both had to endure a "making over" process for 365 days. "Before a young woman's turn came to go in to King Xerxes, she had to complete twelve months of beauty treatments" (Esther 2:12 NIV). In my case the beauty treatments that I received were a cleansing of my sins, a toning of my spirit and a moisturizing (saturation) of God's presence in my life.

Is A Sabbatical Right For You?

The answer is simple, yes! If you are in need of an answer from God, you need a clear head and heart. Think back to the way things were done in the Bible days, how every seventh year was known as the sabbatical year and how debts were canceled and slaves were granted freedom.

> *"When the neighboring peoples bring merchandise or grain to sell on the Sabbath, we will not buy from them on the Sabbath or on any holy day. Every seventh year we will forgo working the land and will cancel all debts" (Neh. 10:31 NIV).*

Truly think about the purpose behind the sabbatical year; it was about renewal and getting rid of the idea of enslavement. How have you been enslaved over the past few years? What has enslaved you? Your husband? Your boyfriend? Your family? Your children? Your career? Your health? Your hobbies? Your shopping habits? Your emotional eating? What things have held you back from accomplishing what God has purposed you to do? Think back to where you were seven years ago. Are you further along? Have you accomplished any of the things that you really needed to accomplish or have you been trying to keep up with the Joneses or playing catch-up? This is your year of freedom, this is the year that God wants to cancel all of your debts and free you from all of your strongholds and distractions. You've got to take the step towards your sabbatical year. You have been laboring and toiling in the fields, but now it's time to rest. It may seem like a daunting task but remember that God won't forsake you; He will be with you every step of the way. Remember Jeremiah's words, "Ah, Sovereign LORD, you have made the heavens and the earth by your great power and outstretched arm. Nothing is too hard for you" (Jeremiah 32:17 NIV). Not even your decision to step out on faith and pursue a sabbatical is too hard for God.

You can't gain this level of sensitivity with a world of distractions. You don't have to announce to the world that you're going on a sabbatical; you just need to decide within yourself how you're going to cut yourself off from distractions, for how long and get started. Everyone around you won't understand, so don't even try to make them, only share your plans to go on a sabbatical with an accountability partner.

Ask a pastor or counselor to suggest some books to read depending on the areas that you are currently struggling with. If you're seeking God for financial peace then you should read books on this topic during your sabbatical. If you're struggling with broken relationships find books to read that will help you to rebuild, not reading material that bashes relationships.

It's also vital that you study God's Word on a regular basis during your sabbatical. Meditate on scriptures that relate to your current need. If you desire to stop fornicating, gambling, gossiping, being lazy or whatever you're battling with, then use a commentary to help you find scripture on these and other topics. Avoid having Bible Studies with friends and family during this time. You don't want someone else's ideology to confuse you or keep you from missing what God has for you and only you. Remember your sabbatical is only for a period of time so the intensity and devotion to God that you have to exhibit will only be for a limited time.

Choosing the time that you need to spend on your sabbatical is solely up to you. Whether you go on a sabbatical for one year, six months, six weeks, or six days, your step of faith is commendable. It takes a woman of faith to surrender all to God, forsaking friends, dating, etc. to encounter an intimate season with God.

Beauty Metamorphosis

During your sabbatical, you will grow in ways that you would have never imagined and your faith will be increased tremendously.

For starters, you will learn more about yourself. You will see yourself the way God sees you and finally experience the genuine joy and peace that you've been searching an eternity for. You will understand the beauty of being you. The purpose that God has given you will be revealed and you will see that His purpose for your life can only be carried out in a way that's unique to your style, your professionalism, your spice, your organizational skills, your flair, your skill level, and your way of getting things done. Your connection to God will be so amazing!

Your special time with God will help you to understand and accept the value of the people around you. The people with a high value who mean you well and have poured into your life purely without motive will be recognized and greatly appreciated. The people who have a low value who are there for a free ride or to stand by in hopes that you will fail will be revealed. The blinders that you have had on your eyes for so long will come off and you will begin to see the true colors of the very people you thought you knew. "And immediately there fell from his eyes something like scales, and he regained his sight." (Acts 9:18). The scales that covered your eyes will fall off and you will regain your spiritual eyesight. You will be able to see exactly who you should befriend, whom you should have relationships with and from whom you need to disassociate yourself. You will realize exactly who and what you need to be connected to and what needs to be a thing of the past. You will begin to develop in the area of boldness and as Proverbs 28:1 (NIV) describes, you will become "as bold as a lion." You might be wondering how you will develop in boldness especially if you've been shy for as long as you remember. A few things may happen. You will be so in love with God that when people ask you about the glow that you have and whether you have a new man in your life, you will gladly tell them yes and go into detail about how good God has been in your life. You won't have to worry about whether your friends will think you're bragging about the favor that God has shown you because you will have weeded out those type of people. You will be in the company of other individuals who experience joy from hearing your testimony. You will be encouraged to share, and in doing so, your boldness to speak will be strengthened for the next opportunity. Another experience that will help you to develop in the area of boldness is by getting involved in your place of worship or with a local ministry. In time you will find yourself talking to complete strangers about God's goodness. You may identify with someone who is standing right where you used to stand and with boldness you will be able to tell them about the time that you took to spend with God. You can encourage someone else that what God did for you, He can and He will do the same for them. "For there is no respect of persons with God" (Rom. 2:11) and God will use whomever makes themselves available to be used. You will be a living testimony!

The closer you get to God, your desires will change, the places you used to go will no longer be of interest to you, the things you used to do will seem so silly. The addictions that you battled with will be overpowered and the strongholds that have kept you at a standstill will be released from your life.

You may have read those last few paragraphs with sheer joy and excitement in anticipation of what you will experience after you take the step to pursue a sabbatical. I encourage you to make a decision right now as to when you will begin your sabbatical and for how long. If you have not already done so stop right now and complete the Self-Evaluation starting on page 119. If you have already completed the self-evaluation, reread what you wrote and take a moment to reflect on how you need to approach your sabbatical and to gauge how long you plan to be on your journey.

Now that you have decided when you will begin your sabbatical, know that your life will change. You have taken the first step to changing your life forever. As you continue to read the rest of this book, you will be enlightened and motivated for your journey. We will explore Esther and why she is the true glamour girl and how she experienced a similar journey. There is also more to come on the lasting results of this amazing new venture that you're about to embark upon. Remember that your experience won't be the same as the next person's and will even be different from when you decide that it's necessary for you to take a second, third or fourth sabbatical. Your experience will be exactly what you need and God's grace, mercy and awesome power will be applied in the areas that you need in order to go to the next level. Pack your Bible, this book, a bottle of water, a great attitude, lots of patience, a compact mirror and plenty of Kleenex. Let's go!

Chapter 8

Esther: The True Glamour Girl

Can you imagine getting facials, hot oil treatments, manicures, pedicures, body massages, and aromatherapy every day for a year? What about being immersed from head to toe in perfumes, drenching your body with moisturizing oils, getting makeup applications and treating your hair with some of the earth's best products for 52 weeks? I don't mean a few weekends out of the year or a couple of days out of the month, I'm talking every single day doing nothing else but enjoy being pampered and beautified constantly. You'd probably say that no one person needs this much attention or has that kind of time and money. Well guess again because this is exactly what took place with Esther and hundreds of other women as they prepared for history's first beauty contest. Sounds exciting, right? It is exciting because whoever won this beauty contest would be chosen as queen. Esther was different from the other contestants not only because of her physical beauty but in other ways as well. Esther didn't let her outer beauty overcompensate for her inner beauty; instead she used both to glorify the true and living God. If you read the book of Esther too fast you will miss some very key points about preparation. Patiently waiting for God to move in your life strengthens your ability to be at your best in all that you do. For you to fully understand the depth of this exciting Bible story, I will take my time in explaining what it was like to be Esther: The True Glamour Girl.

The Truth About the Hidden

One mention of the Book of Esther to Biblical scholars and the focus will quickly turn to the fact that God's name is nowhere to be found in the entire book. However, this somewhat unusual book has the presence of God interwoven throughout each and every chapter. Even though God's name is not mentioned, He is revealed as the one who is hidden. God has strategically hidden his face from the Persians in the Book of Esther and that's exactly how God intended it. The Hebrew phrase for "The Scroll of Esther" means "revelation of the hidden." So even Esther's purpose and identity is hidden until the perfect time for it to be revealed and you know that God is always on time! There are all sorts of hidden devices in the Book of Esther, including and especially the 12-month purification process that she and other virgins had to endure upon going before the king in order to be chosen as queen. Not only did God use divine providence to reach the Persians and Jews in this biblical text, but He also provided for Esther in ways that only He could before, during, and after her rise to become queen. What is hidden does not always mean a lack of presence. As it is revealed in the Book of Esther that which is hidden possesses such an extraordinary depth of power that when it does come to pass it is unexplainable. All that you or anybody else can say is, "God did it."

You may have a gift inside of you that is yet to come to pass because God is still working on you in a lot of ways. Don't get discouraged; just be still. Don't get ahead of God because what He has in you is going to save so many lost souls and ultimately save His people. As we meditate on the Book of Esther we will see how He used Esther for those same reasons.

Search for a New Queen

King Ahasuerus had encountered several victories during his reign as king but he seemed to be having great difficulty in his personal life. After giving a grand party during the third year of his reign that lasted for months on end, he was brought back to reality by a swift blow from his wife. Queen Vashti had been having a party of her own, and when she received word that her husband had sent for her she refused, knowing that he and his guests were probably highly inebriated. When the king caught light of the situation he was instructed by his cabinet of wise men to dethrone Queen Vashti. Although the queen had a right to refuse to go before her husband in his condition, it was a bad mark against her; it made the king seem as if he weren't the head, and it may have caused other women to disobey their husbands as well. King Ahaseurus couldn't allow any confusion in his kingdom and he dethroned Queen Vashti. This is when he began his search for a new queen.

In some years prior to the search for a new queen a man by the name of Mordecai was deported from Jerusalem to Persia. He ended up adopting Esther, his cousin, as his own daughter after her parents' death by the hands of King Nebuchadnezzar. As Esther's Hebrew name means "star" she was befittingly described as fair and beautiful.

When Mordecai heard of the beauty contest being conducted by the king he was eager to learn more. After deciding that this was the ideal event for Esther, Mordecai was elated. He was more than willing to take the risk of Esther being forced to become a concubine if she was not chosen as queen. However, Mordecai was convinced that Esther would win the beauty contest without any problems.

> So it came to pass, when the king's commandment and his decree was heard, and when many maidens were gathered together unto Shushan the palace, to the custody of Hegai, that Esther was brought also unto the king's house, to the custody of Hegai, keeper of the women. (Esther 2:8)

Mordecai did not hesitate; he took his cousin Esther to Hegai, the man that would keep watch over all of the women while preparing to go before the king. Upon entering the palace where the women had to stay, Esther received favor with Hegai. Ultimately, Esther was receiving favor from God who controlled the entire string of events. With the favor that she received from Hegai, Esther was given everything that she needed in order to make her even more beautiful.

Through all the favoritism, Mordecai warned Esther to keep their background and nationality quiet until a later time. Some years prior, Esther's parents had been slain by King Nebuchadnezzar when he overtook the city of Jerusalem. Mordecai adopted Esther and raised her as his own daughter in Persia. With that in the back of his mind, Mordecai was deeply concerned about Esther while she was away at the palace. He went everyday to check on her to make sure that she was safe. Mordecai had forgotten that God saw fit for Esther to receive favor with the keeper of the women and that she had received the best place in the house. So he really did not have a thing to worry about, not then, and not for a while.

Rules of the Contest

Modern day beauty contests seem glamorous with beautiful young women full of unique and sometimes unusual talents; they also express opinions vying for a chance to represent their local counties or even their countries. Nevertheless, before all the lights and cameras flash there are always rules and regulations that must be in order. Even Esther and her opponents had rules to follow before going to see the king. Failing to abide by the rules could cost either of them their chance to sit on the throne. Instead they could be reduced to being a concubine in a harem for the king and neither of them wanted that awful fate.

Now when every maid's turn was come to go in to king Ahasuerus, after that she had been twelve months, according to the manner of women, (for so were the days of their purifications accomplished, to wit, six months with oil of myrrh, and six months with sweet odours, and with other things for the purifying of the women; (Esther 2:12 KJV)

If the scripture above is read too quickly you may miss the fact that Esther and the other "maids" had to spend a total of 12 months involved in a purification process — six months with the oil of myrrh and another six months with sweet odours and other things used for purification. What in the world were these ladies doing for 365 days? Before proceeding to the next verses and the events that occur, let's just pause here for a minute and explore exactly what happened during that entire year with the oil of myrrh and the sweet odours.

Six Months of Oil of Myrrh

For the first six months of the purification process that was ordered by the king the women had to endure the oil of myrrh, which was used in many occasions throughout the Bible. It was used for anointing oil (Exod. 30:23), in perfume (Ps. 45:8, Prov. 7:17, and Songs 3:6), as a gift to baby Jesus (Matt. 2:11), as an offering to Jesus on the cross (Mark 15:23), and it was used to prepare Jesus' body for burial after his death on the cross (John 19:39). In this case the myrrh was used for purification before the maids would be allowed to go before the king in his search for a new queen.

The total of six months that the ladies had to endure the oil of myrrh was a direct symbol of Christ's sufferings. It probably was not an easy task to smell the same fragrance for six months straight. We get tired of the same perfume after only a few weeks. Can you imagine smelling the same fragrance everyday for six months? Well Christ suffered a great deal in order to give Christians the opportunity to receive eternal life. Therefore the maids had to endure some uneasy predicaments in order to qualify for the chance to be queen. The maids had to completely submerge themselves with myrrh for six months. The following is an example of the actual procedures:

> *In this time period, women would build a small charcoal fire in a pit on the floor. A fragrant oil, such as myrrh, sandalwood, etc., would be placed in a cosmetic burner and heated in the fire (purification). The women would crouch naked (totally exposed) over the burner with her robe draped over her head and body to form a tent (booth or tabernacle). As she perspired (ridding of self), her open pores absorbed the fragrance of the oil (Christ). By the time the fire burned out, her skin and clothing would be thoroughly perfumed! (Tanner 2003)*

After a few days, being completely submerged in a wonderful smelling perfume had to seem unexciting to some women. During Esther's experience of becoming purified she had to be truly meek and humble to stay focused on her goal. Esther had to endure a time of suffering so she could really appreciate what God was about to bring her into. Instead of complaining about the monotonous routine, Esther probably spent her days meditating on future events. She probably reflected on her nationality and why Mordecai had asked her to deny it until a later time. She probably wondered where her present state was going to lead her in the future.

The Bible does not say whether some women dropped out of the race because they couldn't follow the rules of the contest. I can imagine that there were some women who complained to the point where they were dismissed. There probably were women who gave up too soon thinking that it was not worth the trouble. Others may have given up just to avoid enduring another day immersed in the oil of myrrh. Esther knew somehow that there was no gain without any pain and suffering.

Six Months of Sweet Odours

For Esther and the other maids who made it through the first six months the time had come for them to endure another six months of purification but this time with sweet odours. To God, sweet odours are nothing more than burnt offerings. In Biblical times when someone built an altar to God and honored Him with a blood sacrifice it was of the highest praise. When blood sacrifices were combined with fire they were considered a sweet odour to God. "And thou shalt *burn* the whole ram upon the altar: it is a *burnt* offering unto the Lord: it is a sweet savour, an offering made by *fire* unto the Lord" (Exodus 29:18 *emphasis mine*).

Esther and the other virgins had to understand that the last six months of the purification process with sweet odours represented total sacrifice, total submission and total reverence-qualities that were required of them before going before the king. At this point you have to wonder who came up with the idea of the yearlong purification process. It did make a lot of sense since these women had to be stronger than the average and these were ways to test their strength. We think of beauty contests as a bunch of beautiful women who advance to the final round by answering a tough question and having great poise all the while. That's not the case as it is written in the book of Esther because it was the very essence of beautification that was used to weed these women out. Esther didn't rise to the top because she enjoyed being pampered in the same oils and perfumes everyday but because she stayed focused. She became one with the fact that all of those things had a much deeper purpose.

Esther's Rise to Becoming Queen

There was one last thing that Esther and the other beauty contestants needed to do before entering into the presence of the king. "Then thus came every maiden unto the king; whatsoever she desired was given her to go with her out of the house of the women unto the king's house" (Esther 2:13). In other words whatever each virgin wanted to take with them to emphasize their beauty or make themselves more desirable was allowed as they went before the king. I can imagine that the women were excited to get this news because some probably could sing, some probably could play an instrument, others probably had an eye for style and chose a nice outfit to wear in the king's presence.

Obviously the women did go before the king with flashy clothes or attempting to display some kind of musical talent because the Scripture says that when Esther went before the king she took nothing.

> "Now when the turn of Esther, the daughter of Abihail, the uncle of Mordecai, who had taken her for his daughter, was come to go in unto the king, she required nothing but what Hegai the king's chamberlain, the

> *keeper of the women, appointed. And Esther obtained*
> *favour in the sight of all them that looked upon her."*
> *(Esther 2:15)*

The other ladies were probably looking at Esther very strangely when she entered the king's house with nothing. However, after a year of purification she was the only one who learned that there wasn't anything more beautiful or more eye-catching than a pure heart. The king could plainly see that Esther was in a state to please him and only him and with nothing more than herself. She did not need to sing a song, do a dance, or flounce around in a royal gown to get his attention. The king had probably seen enough of that in his lifetime. However, it was a pure heart that would not only benefit the king in having a new queen but it would also fulfill God's purpose. Esther was positioned by divine providence to become the new queen and the end of the chapter in Esther soon reveals her hidden talents as God works through her to save the Jews. Not by her own power was Esther able to do these things but by the power of God.

God is God all by Himself and He does not need our help. All He asks is that we make ourselves available. He knows that we are capable because He gives us the power and the ability. The point is, are we available? Are we willing to take time out of our busy lives to prepare as Esther did? Are we so self-absorbed and preoccupied that we can't go through the fire for our Lord and Savior? He sacrificed His life for us so that we might be free from the burden of sin. Knowing and believing that He loved us that much should be more than enough.

A Step Further

When analyzing the Book of Esther it is wise to look at the spiritual message that unfolds within the text. God is trying to reveal something phenomenal through this unique and powerful woman named Esther. She was chosen in a strange way in order to be positioned to carry out God's will because the women who did not become queen had to become concubines. When God leads you to a position or to a place, it is in your best interest to just go. You may not have a backup plan or anyone to support you but that is when you must trust God the most and that is exactly how He will get the glory. When Esther faced a big chance of failing she persevered. She did all that was required of her before entering to meet the king. She showed her ability to be submissive to rules and that is very important. God wants to know that we, like Esther, have what it takes to follow simple rules. It may not always be comfortable or glamorous but neither was the case when Jesus died on the cross to save all sinners.

I am quite sure that the other women looked at Esther during the purification process and thought that they stood as great of a chance as she did to be queen. There was not a guarantee during those 12 months that Esther would be queen and she had to probably endure snide remarks and hateful looks from her competitors. The person chosen by God will always have to endure hardships and tribulations. However, if you make yourself available to God then the good days will certainly outweigh the bad. So whatever grief

Esther endured during those 12 months from the other contestants was not important once she was chosen as queen.

The first six months of the oil of myrrh represented the suffering that Christ himself endured for the sake of sinners. If we want to see the King and be pleasing in His sight, we have to be willing to suffer just as He did for us. We may not have to be nailed to a cross but we may have to lose a few friends or change the way we dress or talk and so on in order to please God.

The next six months of the sweet odours represents the total and complete sacrifice of our lives. This shows God that not only will we suffer for His namesake but we are willing to completely submit ourselves in His name. Everyone wants respect whether it is from parents, husbands and wives, elders, etc. so of course the true and living King deserves the utmost respect. He wants to know that His followers will submit themselves to Him.

The entire point of the Book of Esther is not so much that she is chosen as queen among all the fair maidens but it is what she does once she sits on the throne. God does not want to simply raise His people to new heights; He wants to fulfill His purpose of saving lost souls to live eternally in His kingdom, which He will do through the works of His faithful people. In the scriptures, Esther represented a Christ-figure because she symbolized salvation. She rose to the occasion and saved her people and God's people. Esther became the bride to the king just as we prepare to become the bride to our King; Esther took the time to prepare to become queen for the king and anyone seeking to obtain favor from the King must take time to prepare also. Preparing to become the bride of the King exudes respect, honor and a great desire to be in God's glory for an eternity. Even today we can prepare for this grand event. We should take into consideration the ways Esther prepared for her groom or think about how modern day brides prepare for their husbands. Most importantly we should do our best to understand what Christ is looking for in a bride.

The Scripture often refers to a bride as being a virgin: someone who was untouched and pure. Therefore God is looking for a bride, which is metaphorically the church, with people who have pure hearts and pure devotion. Comparable to the way Esther's pure nature allowed her to save God's people, we can have a positive effect on the world and more souls will be saved if we follow God's word.

The Big Day

All across the world women have ways of preparing for their wedding day. The bride to be must prepare spiritually, mentally, physically, emotionally, and financially. The most important of these to God, however, is preparing spiritually. This is the area where the bride learns about Christ's love for the church, how she represents the church and how her bridegroom represents God. Both men and women can learn about God's love for His people through the symbolism of a bride and a groom. Both the husband and wife trust that they are marrying a person with a pure heart. They believe that person will be there through sickness and health, for better or for worse and until death. In the same sense, Christ wants us to be in a place where we can come to Him with a pure heart so that He can use us to the best of our ability. Otherwise, we will find ourselves caught in the trap of what man sees as important. Man-made goods such as fancy cars, jewels, and other material items are worthless if we do not recognize God as the true King. God certainly does not want to see His people fail but the choice is up to us. Can God use you as a vessel like He used Esther? The cost of allowing God to have His way in your life may seem high but in the end it will prove to be priceless. Even if you are not engaged or you have yet to prepare for that "big day" there's a bigger day for which we all must prepare. That's the day when each of us will finally get to see our True Love, our True King.

Chapter 9

The Master Artist

Every makeup artist strives to be at the top of his or her game by staying abreast of all the latest techniques, tools and trends in makeup. However, no matter how excellent even the most experienced makeup artist may be, he or she will never be able to top the Master Artist — Jesus. Makeup artists have the skills to change your look on the outside. They can make your nose look smaller or your eyes look bigger. They can take you from drab to fab in a matter of minutes. All those makeup effects are great; however, only Jesus has the power to dramatically change you in a way that a makeup artist could only visualize. In Psalm 51:10, David asked of God, "create in me a pure heart, O God, and renew a steadfast spirit within me." What makeup artist can create in you a pure heart? Sure, they can make your acne scars and blemishes go away for one night but they can't give you a pure heart. What makeup artist can give you a steadfast spirit? Sure, they can make you commit to buying their products on a consistent basis by selling you on all of the benefits and making you feel as those you can't live a day without their products but those makeup artists can't help you to be faithful or to choose right over wrong. Only your Master Artist, the One who created you, can do that!

Don't spend half of your life trying to find other people to understand you and tell you exactly what you want to hear. Don't waste energy hoping and wishing that you will meet someone who has gone through exactly what you've gone through or currently experiencing. You may never find that someone but you do have a Savior who knows everything about you, more than any stranger or close friend knows. He knows the number of "the very hairs of your head" (Matt. 10:30). A close friend or the person that you're seeking to tell you all about your life would never even take the time to count the number of hairs on your head, so stop looking for that in a person! Instead lift your eyes "unto the hills, from whence cometh [your] help" (Ps. 121:1). Most importantly, turn your search toward heaven! Everyday I encourage you to "press on toward the mark for the prize of the high calling of God in Christ Jesus" (Phil. 3:14). Seek out the presence of God; seek out the One who truly seeks you.

The Ultimate Makeover

There's nothing like a relaxing massage, a fresh manicure and pedicure, a full face of makeup, a new hairdo, a lovely fragrance or a dazzling new outfit. All these things make us feel pulled together and glamorous. We walk with our heads a little higher and with a little more pep in our step. So what's the drawback? The feelings that those things give us don't last for long. We forget about our massage as soon as we return to work. Our manicure doesn't last past the dishes. We can't really show off our pedicure at work due to the closed-toe shoe policy. One good workout and our hairstyle is gone. We can't smell our new fragrance over the smell of Pine-

Sol and other household cleaning products, and when we check our budget we may have to return that new outfit we bought.

The best makeover that you can receive is given by the one who specializes in ultimate makeovers. There used to be a reality show called Swan where the host along with plastic surgeons and image consultants would choose a person and dramatically change their outer appearance. I often wondered what happened to those people psychologically after all the attention they were receiving from doctors, makeup artists, fashion designers, etc., ceased to exist. I wondered how these people really felt about themselves deep down on the inside now that there was no one there to convince them that they were beautiful. Don't get me wrong if someone has a chipped tooth, or a badly shaped nose from a car accident then they should get that surgically fixed if they can afford to do so. Nevertheless, plastic surgery doesn't change self-esteem issues; at least I don't think it does.

The only way that you can fix your self-esteem issues is to look within. Even after reading this book and tons of other self-help books, if you fail to take the steps to figure out what's holding you back, then your problems will never be solved. The first step to boosting your self-esteem is understanding that you are your biggest problem and that you are standing in your own way of being successful and experiencing all that life has to offer. It almost seems like you have to tear yourself down in order to build yourself back up. But isn't that what builders do when they decide to rebuild? Change your perspective! You're not tearing yourself down but instead you're tearing down your own attitudes of defeat, envy toward others, self-hatred, degradation and so on. It's the necessary process to rebuilding your life and your way of seeing yourself. Until you take the time to face yourself and begin the process of tearing down the issues that are holding you back, you will continue to go through life being unhappy with yourself which leads to unhappiness toward others. You've heard the saying, "Hurt people, hurt people" so love yourself so you can begin to truly love others.

Chapter 10

Pleased With The Results

You are finished with your sabbatical and now the real work begins. You've evolved and others haven't, you've gotten closer to God and others seem to be straying farther away, and you have discovered your purpose while others seem to still be struggling with why they are in this world. So now what? It's time for you to take a deep breath and pack your bags for a journey down a path that may be filled with less people and seemingly less fun things to do. Your attention has to be on doing what you've been purposed to do. If your purpose seems to be something that you dread, then you may need to re-read the earlier chapters of this book.

Your choice to walk the straight and narrow should be one that's pleasing, coupled with a feeling of peace. There will be times when you may feel perplexed and unhappy because you seem so different from everyone else or so distant from everyone else, but those feelings are tricks of the enemy to steal your peace or to confuse you. Satan doesn't want you to know your purpose, let alone have peace about what God has called you to do, so Satan will operate through friends, family co-workers, etc., with tricks of jealousy, envy, competition, or lack of support. Satan won't stop there; he will even attack you through your own personal issues such as baggage from your past, fear, financial roadblocks, poor self-confidence, etc. to deter you. All those things will make you forget about all the progress that you've made and if you give in, it will rob you of your peace and your purpose. Ask God to keep you in perfect peace. The kind of peace that affirms you, that without a shadow of a doubt, you are walking boldly in your purpose. It's the type of peace that surpasses all levels of understanding in the natural realm. "And the peace of God, which transcends all understanding, will guard your hearts and your minds in Christ Jesus" (Phil. 4:7 NIV). This type of peace will help you go to sleep at night and get just the right amount of beauty rest, one without worry, frustration, or regret.

Your sabbatical experience is a journey that you won't want to trade for anything in the world. As long as you keep allowing God to go before you as a banner and as long as you position yourself to go forth as God instructs you from day to day, you will be extremely pleased with the results. You will be in awe of the blessings that will begin to manifest in your life and the people who are connected to you. For example, this book is a result of my sabbatical experience and by reading this book you have connected yourself to my blessings and I'm connected to your blessings. I am purposed to equip you with what you need to be all that you were created to be, and because of that lives will be blessed through us. It's a cycle, it's a sisterhood, and it's a privilege.

After your sabbatical experience, you will begin to see and feel the results in a dramatic almost out-of-body type of way. You may make the decision to leave Corporate America and go into full-time ministry. You may find yourself packing up and moving to another city or country so that you can serve God in more of a leadership capacity. You may take the step to cut certain things and certain people out of your life to avoid being distracted any longer from God's will. You're changing; you're coming into who you were created to be. Life seems so different. God is bringing new people and new opportunities into your life at such a rapid pace and you don't know how you even arrived at your current destination. Well let me remind you! You've experienced God on such an intense level because you made a commitment to do so. The results are mind-blowing and guess what? God will continue to bless you and favor you. The beauty that you now possess after your sabbatical experience is the kind that God adores, the kind that can be seen from the inside out. It's boldness, it's excitement, it's awesomeness, it's thankfulness, and it's a yearning to do God's will. Boldness, Excitement, Awesomeness, Thankfulness, and a Yearning to do God's Will, now that's B.E.A.U.T.Y.!

Notes

Chapter 11

The Beauty of It All

The relationships that we have with God and the other people in our lives are vital to our survival and the people surrounding us. Healthy relationships bring happiness and insurmountable peace into your life. The beauty of it all is that you have figured out what your purpose is in life through your sabbatical and now you know the type of influence that you should have with other people and you can move forward in making an impact in your home, your community and the nation. Let's explore how to maintain healthy relationships with different people in your life.

You and God

Your relationship with God is the most important relationship that you should have in your life. If you are mature enough to develop and maintain your relationship with God from a young age then you are miles ahead of many. However, if you're like most people you've spent far too much time on the wrong roads in life investing in other people first and going to God last. Doing so is like being birthed by your mother and after your umbilical cord is cut you immediately jump out of the incubator, put on your business attire, grab a suitcase and go to work without ever thanking your mother for carrying you and birthing you.

God is your Creator and it's a beautiful thing to take the time to get know the person who knit you together in your mother's womb, to find out why He created you to go the places that you will go and to be the person that you are destined to be. Why go through life as though you had anything to do with who you are and where you're going? The moment you feel like you have what you have — a degree, a husband, children, nice house, nice clothes, car, boat, wealth, etc. — because of something that you did, is the very moment that you've stepped outside of God's will. Always remember, "He causes his sun to rise on the evil and the good, and sends rain on the righteous and the unrighteous" (Matt. 5:45 NIV). Therefore, you're no better in having great things than a drug lord who has obtained nice things. If neither person acknowledges God for who He is and neither person lives a life free of sin then unfortunately there is no difference. However, God still has sufficient grace and mercy on everyone, even those who are living outside of His will.

All About You

You must learn to have a healthy relationship with yourself whether you're single, married, a parent/guardian, etc. Learn to do the things that make you happy. What makes you laugh? Is it watching old episodes of *Friends* or *Everybody Loves Raymond*? Is it looking at funny videos online? Is it flipping through old photo albums? What makes you cry? Watching Lifetime movies, listening to music from your youth, or someone not being dependable? What makes you angry? Someone leaving one drop of milk in the carton, a rude co-worker or a poor driver? The list could go on and on and you should know what things lead to certain emotions. You should know what you should do when you're faced with tough situations in life so that you don't overheat or have a nervous breakdown. You as an individual are not that complicated. If you take the time to get to know yourself inside and out then half the battle is won.

In addition, do the things that make you who you are — go window shopping, get a pedicure, help a friend organize their closet, book a vacation with the girls, go to the park with the kids or whatever you enjoy doing! For me, it's lying on the couch for hours on end looking at music videos, baking and eating oatmeal raisin cookies, talking on the phone to my big sister and being lazy. That's something that I have to do for myself at least once a month, no work, no business-related phone calls, no entertaining the mini-me or solving problems. Once my ME day is over, it's back to fulfilling my many roles in life. I have some friends who love to shop or get a massage on their ME day. For some it's spending time with their children or inviting others over for a homemade dinner. You have to know what makes YOU happy and tap into that once or twice a month. This is the only way that you can truly be an excellent individual, daughter, wife, mother, sister, aunt, neighbor, boss, employee, (fill in the blanks) _____, _____, _____, _____, _____.

You and Your Spouse

Marriage is such a beautiful ministry and a privilege for those who have taken that step. When you approach marriage as a ministry, you understand the importance of keeping it going strong and with pure excellence. Think about the ministries at your place of worship or in your local community, the ones that have lasted for years and the ones that need serious help. The ministries that have successfully lasted for years are the ones that focused on their mission and worked hard year in and year out to step it up a notch bringing in more programs, utilizing strategies that work, constantly gaining knowledge, using state-of-the art technology and so on. The ministries that need serious help are those that don't have effective leaders, lack of support from members and other stakeholders, poor vision, no creativity, failure to get assistance, unsuccessful marketing and so on.

Marriage is the same way; the ones that work are the ones where the parties involved do all that they can to keep it afloat. When they've mastered one area, they move on to master another area and another and another. They seek out mentors to help them through difficult seasons, they do what it takes to keep the marriage spicy or cutting edge, they read books (Bible, Self-Help, Relationship, etc.) to continue gaining knowledge, and they market the marriage well by letting others know that they are happily married to prevent infidelity, jealousy and other destroying vices. Marriages that don't have success are those with two people that get to a point where they fail to make any effort to keep the ministry going. A laissez faire approach is taken to improving the communication in the ministry, choosing people (or not) to help the ministry improve, and showing no interest in reviving any of the dead or near dead areas of the ministry. Before long this type of marriage has lost hope and is in serious need of help.

All the Single Ladies: If you desire to be married you are in such a great position to learn from your married friends. Many of them have no clue what they're doing and that's not necessarily a bad thing because you will be there one day. Married couples have to trust God with blind faith just as we have to do with any new situation. However, you can glean from a married couple's errors and not do the same. I even watch the show *Divorce Court* just to avoid making some of the same mistakes that I see couples trying to get out of on nationwide television. So instead of moping around wondering where your mate is, spend time praying mightily for your married family and friends and treat the situation that you're in as learning ground. Sow into your married friends and family's lives by purchasing them helpful books, babysitting their kids so they can have a date night, celebrating their anniversaries with cards and praise, and extending ongoing encouragement. You will be surprised how much you are learning and you will reap a great reward for sowing into their ministry.

The best way to ensure that you and your spouse have a happy medium is to: 1) have a great relationship with God to understand your role as an individual and as a wife or future wife; 2) have a great relationship with yourself so that you understand when you need to have a ME day so that you can be a submissive and respectable wife at all times. In addition, remember the three C's: Communicate, Collaborate and Consummate. Always communicate even when your spouse doesn't know what to say or refuses to say anything at all. Remember when to go to God and when to vent to your friends and family. Be sure to collaborate on as many things as possible. I love to see married couples doing things together — serving at church, performing community service, running marathons, conducting Bible study, organizing book clubs, singing, cooking, dancing and so on. ALWAYS have something that you do with your husband that is unique to any other relationships that you maintain. You may play the Wii or X-box with the kids, or sing in the choir with your neighbor or swap recipes with your co-workers, but you and your husband should be salsa dancing every Friday night or hosting dinner parties where you both do the cooking or traveling the world and keeping a log of where you go and what you do. Make it exciting and make it a collaborative effort that no one else can replace. Lastly, consummate your marriage often. This shouldn't just happen once or twice just to make the marriage official. It should happen often as a symbol of the fact that you're happily married. Trust me, your single friends would give their left arm for this privilege so take an Excedrin for the headache, get plenty of rest and exercise, cut the telephone and television off and remind your husband often of one of the reasons why he married you!

You and Your Children

The most precious gifts from God are children. You know this to be a fact because you are indeed a precious gift to your parents, grandparents, step-parents or guardians. If you are reading this book, your caretakers made time to give you a great start in life and you owe that much to your parents. No matter how your relationship changed over the years or the trials that tested your relationship, always be respectful and appreciative of the fact that you exist.

Parents have the awesome privilege of shaping their children from birth to adulthood and to teach them the right way to go in life. Any mistakes that parents made in their lives can be corrected through their offspring; generational curses can be broken and better opportunities can be provided. Parents have experienced the results of both good and poor choices and can ensure that their children are aware of the paths to take in life. Ephesians 6:4 instructs parents to raise their children "up in the nurture and admonition of the Lord." If you noticed or even imagined an unruly, disrespectful child then you would understand why parents need to have guidelines on how to raise children. In order for children to be brought up in the admonition of Christ some ingredients need to be set in place. If you are a parent/guardian now or you desire to be one in the future, you've got to: 1) have a great relationship with God to understand your role as a parent or future parent, so you can hear from the Holy Spirit regarding who to seek for counsel and other assistance; 2) have a great relationship with yourself so that you understand when you need to have a ME day because your duties as a parent will become overwhelming at one point or another.

Your relationship with your child is not rocket science. It's easy if you make it easy and it's hard if you make it hard. Create balance with your child early on as well as boundaries. Having balance is healthy because you had a life before you became a parent so it's not wise to forfeit the things that make you happy and make you the unique person that you are. When you are out of balance, you can't be the parent that you need to be anyway because you are carrying around frustration and resentment which can lead to anger or even depression. By the way, if you're experiencing any of those emotions then your life is out of balance. You hold the key to get it back in balance.

Create boundaries between you and your children so they understand who the parent is and who the child is. Also create boundaries on who's allowed to give advice to you regarding your child. Lastly, create boundaries regarding activities that children are involved in, the company they keep, the places they go, the shows they watch, the music they listen to, etc. This is where having a strong relationship with God comes in because if you're getting bad advice that doesn't line up with the Word of God then it's not the advice for you. If your children feel they are capable of making their own choices and become more and more rebellious by the day then it's time to place them on the altar to establish boundaries. God expects us to pray and fall on our faces before Him for everything, parenting skills is no exception. Ask God to show you how to be a parent, who to seek for advice, and how to raise your children up right. You will begin to see God moving on your behalf and placing people in your life to advise and assist you. John 10:10 reminds us that the thief "comes only to steal, and to kill, and to destroy" and Satan lurks 24 hours a day seeking whose child he can claim. Don't give up the fight for your children. Instead, strive daily as a parent to have balance so you can be a healthy parent spiritually, physically, mentally, and emotionally. Remember to also create boundaries so you can spend less time running yourself ragged listening to everyone else's opinions on how to raise your child, ripping and running to please your child and neglecting every opportunity that you have to instruct your child on how to be a powerful man/woman of God. With the help of God, you have all the potential to be an awesome parent. It's never too late to work on the relationship between you and your child.

You and Your Friends

My pastor often reminds the congregation that we must do life together. Those three words — do life together — speak volumes for the purpose of friendship. Real friends are like sisters from another mister and brothers from another mother; they are so much like family because you have similar DNA and doing life together is a breeze. People come in and out of our lives but not everyone deserves the title of friend. I know you've heard the saying, "Some people are in your life for a reason or a season or a lifetime." In order to spot the roles that people play in your life you need to first have a great relationship with God so that you can develop a discerning spirit about the genuineness of a person. Then, have a great relationship with yourself so that you understand what you need in a friend and what you don't need and when it's okay to cut ties with friends who may be toxic.

Now you might be thinking to yourself, "What is a toxic friend?" It's sort of an oxymoron because you wouldn't call a friend toxic, would you? It seems that anything that is toxic can't be good. Think about toxic waste dumps or when you visit the doctor and they discard needles and other items in containers labeled toxic. In essence, a toxic friend is someone that can and will cause harm in your life. Let's explore a few toxic situations among so-called friends:

Toxic Situation 1

After a couple of bad experiences, Amy reluctantly decided to go to a party with her friend Bethany. Amy expressed to Bethany beforehand that they should stay together and watch each other's back. Bethany reassures Amy that no one will bother them at the party and everything will be okay. As soon as the two enter the party, Bethany disappears with a guy into a dark corner. Later Amy sees Bethany taking shots of liquor with a group of strangers. Amy tries to get Bethany to leave the party. Bethany claims that she is okay and that they would leave soon. Amy keeps a close eye on Bethany but is distracted by a fight that breaks out. When Amy is clear from danger she searches frantically to find a non-existent Bethany. Amy resorts to sitting in her car hoping that Bethany would soon appear. After a few hours, Amy sees a couple of guys carrying out an apparently drunk girl. When Amy realizes that the girl is Bethany she rescues her from the guys in fear of what they had in mind. The next weekend, Amy receives a phone call from Bethany who wants to go to another party. What should Amy do?

Toxic Situation 2

Christopher has been involved with his new girlfriend for about three months. His friend Jason is known to be a bit of a ladies' man and has a reputation. Christopher doesn't pay attention to the rumors that he has heard about his friend Jason. On one occasion Christopher needed Jason to pick his girlfriend up from the airport. Jason was happy to help and put on his best outfit and favorite cologne and headed to the airport. When Jason arrived, Christopher's girlfriend April noticed how strangely Jason was acting. Jason used every possible opportunity to stand a little too close to April or flash his winning smile. Everything that Jason did made April extremely uncomfortable. When April was home, she called Christopher to explain the situation. Christopher refused to believe that his friend of 8 years would try to flirt with his girlfriend. Who should he believe?

Sometimes it's hard to pinpoint a toxic friend and it's even harder to end this type of friendship. Therefore, in choosing friends consider what Jesus said in John 15:12: "This is my commandment, That ye love one another, as I have loved you." So you should love your friends as Christ has loved you and your friends should do the same. In any situation if a so-called friend does not have your best interest at heart then that person is a toxic friend. If you continue to deal with that person they will soon get you into a situation that can be dangerous to your life.

Always keep your eyes open and your hand in God's hand to recognize warning signs of toxic friendships. I Corinthians 10:13

reminds us that "There hath no temptation taken you but such as is common to man: but God is faithful, who will not suffer you to be tempted that ye are able; but will with the temptation also make a way of escape, that ye may be able to bear it." In other words, God always gives us a way out especially in toxic friendships. In each situation that was mentioned, there were warning signs for the characters to steer clear of their toxic friends.

God will not choose your friends for you so when people come into your life use your best judgment. Choose wisely! If you struggle to find friends or you've been hurt too many times before, remember to "seek first his kingdom and his righteousness, and all these things will be given to you as well" (Matt. 6:33 NIV). There are no exceptions to what God will give you; He will give you true friends. So trust God and look for Him in the people that come into your life as you make choices of who to befriend. If you fail, God will always help you to pick up the pieces.

Every relationship that you have in your life should be prioritized based on importance. The top two healthy relationships should be with God and yourself. If you have those two relationships intact every other relationship will fall in place as healthy and thriving. However, if you neglect God and disrespect His place in your life you are surely headed for demise. Likewise, if you fail to value your own self — mentally, physically, and emotionally — you are on a downward spiral to breakdowns, health issues and/or depression. When you find yourself spinning out of control pull this book out and re-read this chapter to get back on the right track.

Chapter 12

Timeless Beauty

As women we have so many hats to wear and so many roles to play. I don't think that anyone has a job that's harder than what it takes to be a woman. What makes our job so tough is that we have to be so many things to so many people, with a smile on our face, raging hormones, mood swings and high heels. I have discovered a well-kept secret that will prevent women from going off the deep end while trying to do all that is required of us. Are you ready to know the secret? Close the doors, turn off the phone, and grab a highlighter! The secret is simply to remember that you are royalty and that you are a daughter of the King. "But you are a chosen people, a royal priesthood, a holy nation, God's special possession, that you may declare the praises of him who called you out of darkness into his wonderful light" (1 Pet. 2:9 NIV). Walk out of the dark places that you've been in; start carrying yourself like the Queen that you are and experience life the way God intended for His children.

Once you accept and start walking in your purpose and you realize that your work is not in vain, what you do in every area of your life will result in eternal rewards. In Luke 18:29-30, Jesus reminds us that "there is no one who has left house or wife or brothers or parents or children for the sake of the kingdom of God who will not receive in return many times more in this world and, in the coming age, eternal life." Imagine if you had to leave your family members behind to take a job in another city or country, attend college, etc., you can understand how hard that would be. Luke 18 is saying that anything that we do, give up, or endure for the kingdom of God will result in the receiving of eternal life. That's great news on those days when it's extra challenging to be a submissive wife, an obedient daughter, a firm mother, a saved single, a faithful leader, a diligent employee and so on. "God will give repay each person according to what they have done. To those who by persistence in doing good seek glory, honor and immortality, he will give eternal life" (Rom. 2:6-8 NIV). Therefore, no matter what hat you have to wear during the 24 hours of a day and 52 weeks of the year, you are a timeless beauty inside and outside because you are fulfilling your purpose on this earth. For that you will gain eternal life, which is the ultimate, timeless beauty benefit.

When you accept who you are as a virtuous woman of God you have immediately set yourself apart from the millions of other women who are still trying to find themselves. Once you are able to honestly say, I love being a Wife, Mom, Youth Leader, Entrepreneur, Soccer Coach or whatever you do on a daily basis, then you become different from the huge percentage of women who complain about every part of their life. Embrace your many roles as a woman and spend less time griping and more time being an example to others. There are plenty of women out there who are standing at the crossroads of life who need your example. If you think back you can remember when you were once there (or you may still be there), when you tried to please everyone but God, when you did what was popular, when you didn't know how to love yourself. Just like you needed someone to inspire you, to remind you of your worth and teach you the keys to happiness, other women still struggling need you to encourage them through your words, your actions and your choices.

Being a timeless beauty isn't easy. Think about it, not everything can hold the title of being timeless or being able to fit in anywhere at any place or time. It takes a special piece of décor to achieve such an effect in a home, a certain type of art to hold this value in a museum or a different type of woman to fit into any crowd without losing who she is. You are a timeless beauty.

Beauty That Never Fades

We must all leave a legacy or our lives are simply worthless and we will be forgotten by future generations. "You are a mist that appears for a little while and then vanishes" (James 4:14 NIV). God did not create us to be worthless or to take up space. Until we leave this earth, we should be busy about God's business and drawing lost souls to Christ. You should no longer wonder how you can make your name great because all you have to do is take a step. You've got to do something that you've never done before in order to experience something that you've never experienced before. God told Abram to leave his country and his family to acquire land. God is not asking us to give up nearly as much as he asked Abram but you've got to be willing to do something so that God can fulfill his promises for your life. "I will make you into a great nation and I will bless you; I will make your name great, and you will be a blessing" (Gen. 12:2 NIV). This is your season to claim what is rightfully yours: nations, blessings and a great name! It won't happen overnight but it will happen in your lifetime if you just take the necessary steps. If you're still wondering what the steps are, read this book from the beginning. Accept Christ into your life as your Lord and Savior, believe that He died on the cross for your sins and rose from the dead with all power and confess it with your mouth and your actions as a follower of Christ. Connect with a local church and place of worship and get planted there so you can continue to learn, grow and go through life with people who will hold you accountable and will encourage you until you see the beauty that you truly possess.

Stay Glamorous!

Self-Discovery: B.E.A.U.T.Y Trends for Self-Improvement

When completing the following activities, look for this beauty icon which indicates a reference to **B.E.A.U.T.Y. Scriptures** that will enhance your ability to _Believe, Expound, Activate, Utilize, Teach_ and _Yearn_ for the messages from God that will launch you into your destiny.

B.E.A.U.T.Y. Scriptures will help you to:

- ☑ **B**elieve the scriptures
- ☑ **E**xpound on the scriptures _(Read different versions/refer to a concordance)_
- ☑ **A**ctivate the scriptures-set them into motion
- ☑ **U**tilize the scriptures in your everyday life
- ☑ **T**each the scriptures to others
- ☑ **Y**earn for the scriptures — read God's word with passion

Woman in the Mirror Activity

"I am fearfully and wonderfully made." Psalm 139:14

For this activity, you should be facing yourself in the mirror, whether you're in the bathroom or using a pocket mirror. You will have some questions to ponder aloud while you're looking at your reflection and on others you will need a pen to jot down your responses.

How would you describe yourself?_____

_____

How would your friends describe you? _____

_____

List 3-5 things that you're good at:_____

_____

_____

How does it make you feel when you can accomplish things?_____

_____

_____

List 3-5 things that you WISH you were good at: _____

_____

_____

How does it make you feel when you fail at things? _____

_____

_____

How do you handle frustration? _____

_____

_____

How would your friends say you handle frustration?_____

_____

_____

List the people who support you most:_____

_____

_____

"As iron sharpens iron, so a man sharpens the countenance of his friend." Proverbs 27:17

Pick one person from your list and talk directly to your reflection in the mirror as if you were talking to that person. Thank him or her, share your appreciation, etc. Don't hold back and take as much time as you need. Repeat with a different person from your list if desired.

"He who covers and forgives an offense seeks love, but he who repeats or harps on a matter separates even close friends." Proverbs 17:9

List the people who have hurt you most: _____

_____

_____

Pick one person from your list and talk directly to your reflection in the mirror as if you were talking to the person who caused the hurt. Explain why, how, when, etc. Don't hold back and take as much time as you need. Repeat with a different person from your list if desired.

Now proceed to answer the following:

Are you firmly planted at a place of worship? _____

Do you study the Word of God on a regular basis? _____

Do you pray and ask God to fulfill your needs? _____

Do you trust that God hears and answers your prayers?_____

Do you serve in your local place of worship?_____

Do you pay your tithes? _____

Do you save money for emergencies? _____

Do you pay all of your bills on time? _____

Do you exercise at least three days per week? _____

Do you serve in your local community on a regular basis? _____

What is your highest level of education? ___High school ___Trade or Vocational School ___College ___Graduate School ___Other

Are you satisfied with your current salary? _____

Are you in a healthy relationship (dating/marriage)? _____

Do you have friends/family who hold you accountable? _____

Do you affirm yourself daily?_____

If you answered no to at least five or more of the above questions, you may need to do some self-evaluating. See below.

What activities do you indulge in that you feel are not pleasing in the sight of God?_____

_____

_____

How can you break the cycle/generational curse? _____

_____

_____

Self-Evaluation

"For I know the plans I have for you," declares the LORD, "plans to prosper you and not to harm you, plans to give you hope and a future." Jeremiah 29:11

How old are you? _____

At your current age what did you think you would've accomplished by now?_____

_____

_____

Who/What has kept you from accomplishing your goals? _____

_____

_____

What is your purpose? _____

_____

_____

If you don't know what your purpose is, what types of things are you good at? What comes to you naturally?_____

_____

_____

TIP: Whatever you are naturally good at, your gift is there. Don't look past your gift any longer.

Where do you see yourself in the next 5 years? _____

_____

_____

The next 10 years? _____

_____

_____

The next 20 years? _____

_____

_____

Who do you have in your life that truly supports your dreams/
goals? _____

_____

_____

TIP: Anyone in your circle that shows the slightest bit of
negativity, doubt and lack of support needs to be kept at a
distance. Pray for them that God will help them to be more
supportive or that He move them out of your path temporarily
(until your goal is accomplished) or permanently.

Do you have what it takes to reach your goals? Why or why not?

_____

_____

_____

Below each category, list a few goals you wish to accomplish:

Spiritual

Financial

Physical

Community Service/Volunteer Work

Career/Education

Relationships

_____(Create Your Own Category)

Accomplishing Your Goals

Write today's date: _____

Write the date one year from today:_____

> *For each goal that you mentioned above, give yourself one year to get it accomplished. In 365 days, you should be able to realistically reach at least one, if not all, of your goals. If Esther was able to endure 365 days to prepare for her position as Queen, surely you can take 365 days to transform into the woman that God has called you to be. You have one year from today's date to meet your goals and you can do it!*

My Accountability Partner

"Therefore confess your sins to each other and pray for each other so that you may be healed. The prayer of a righteous man is powerful and effective." James 5:16

Throughout this book having an accountability partner is suggested often and is highly recommended. An accountability partner is someone who is in a pure and strong relationship with God, who can pray with you, advise you, encourage you and support you during the different phases of your current season. You may not always have the same accountability partner during every season of your life and the goal is that you become strong and pure in your relationship with God so you can be an accountability partner to someone who needs you. So how can you know if you're ready to have an accountability partner? How do you know if the person that you'd like to partner with is capable of holding you accountable? Are you capable of holding someone else accountable? Complete the questions below and this should give you a better understanding.

> *"For where two or three come together in my name, there am I with them." Matthew 18:20*

List the things YOU think an accountability partner should do.

_____

_____

_____

In what ways can you realistically provide someone with the same things that you expect of an accountability partner? _____

_____

_____

Name the person with potential to be your accountability partner.

_____

Why did you choose this person? _____

_____

_____

Are you willing to open up with this person? Explain why or why not. _____

_____

_____

Are you strong enough to share mistakes that you've made with your accountability partner? Explain why or why not? _____

_____

_____

Having an accountability partner is a courageous and bold step. It definitely takes time and your act of faith will be greatly rewarded. We'd all like to have someone who looks out for us and God has put virtuous women (and Godly men) on this earth to connect with you. Allow yourself to be vulnerable for a season for the benefits of leading a disciplined yet fulfilled life. If you don't already have an accountability partner, take time this week to seek God to send someone your way or to open your eyes to recognize the person that He has already sent into your life.

Defining Your Self-Esteem

"You are altogether beautiful, my love; there is no flaw in you." Song of Solomon 4:7
Read each question and circle or place a mark by your answer. Be honest so you can get a true reflection of how you view yourself.

1. All of your friends are in relationships and always talk about their romantic dates, their affection for their mate and so on, you
   a. are happy for them but focus on more important things in your life.
   b. lie about different people that you have met.

   c. date people with no substance just to have someone to talk about.

2. Your expensive heirloom is missing and all the facts point to your significant other, you

   a. dismiss them immediately; you can do bad by yourself.

   b. steal something of theirs to even the score.

   c. confront them about it, but then act like nothing ever happened.

3. You go shopping for a trendy new outfit that you saw, but nothing looks right on you, you

   a. decide not to go out, but sit at home and complain.

   b. just look for something that does compliment you or wear something that you already own.

   c. wear anything whether it's appropriate or not just to buy something new.

4. Your friends try to set you up with someone and you find out that they are not interested, you

   a. move on because you can't please everyone.

   b. mope for weeks wondering what's wrong with you or them.

   c. stalk them and make them see your beauty.

5. Time is moving on and you can't decide what to do: go to school or work that dead-end job. You

   a. seek guidance from counselors, friends or parents, then make necessary changes.

   b. just take classes so you can say you're in college but you really don't have a particular goal.

   c. quit your job and lose motivation to go to school.

6. Your high school reunion is in a month. You
   a. regret your life and decide not to go.
   b. are thrilled at the chance to see your old friends.
   c. go just to see who looks the best after 10 years.

7. Your job wants to offer you a position in your favorite city, you
   a. decide that you won't take the job in fear of leaving your friends/family.
   b. jump at the chance and the wonderful opportunity.
   c. worry about what job opportunities your other co-workers will be offered.

Now let's see how you measure up!

"But you are a chosen race, a royal priesthood, a holy nation, a people for his own possession, that you may proclaim the excellencies of him who called you out of darkness into his marvelous light." I Peter 2:9

Check the value of your answer based on how you answered the questions above. (Don't cheat!)

1. a.) 4   b.) 2   c.) 3
2. a.) 4   b.) 3   c.) 2
3. a.) 2   b.) 4   c.) 3
4. a.) 4   b.) 2   c.) 3
5. a.) 4   b.) 3   c.) 2
6. a.) 2   b.) 4   c.) 3
7. a.) 2   b.) 4   c.) 3

TOTAL_____

Results

25-30

You have a very high level of self-esteem. You know what you want out of life and no one can stop you. The harder someone tries to stop you the harder you push. You are not afraid of opportunity and you are eager to tackle any given task. You are not easily upset by failure. You have a wonderful sense of self and motivation for everyday living. Keep up the positive attitude even when storms come in your life. Be sure to fulfill your purpose, walk in your destiny and while you're at it, spread your joy and great outlook on life with others.

15-24

You are somewhat in between having a high level of self-esteem and having low self-esteem. You have the potential to do great things, but are sometimes held back because you worry about what other people think of you and your decisions. You are wishy-washy at times when you should be vigilant. This may lead to low levels of self-esteem for extended periods if you are not careful. In order to stay on the higher end of self-esteem you need to know that you have a purpose and that your destiny is waiting for you. Change your attitude and get busy!

0-14

You, unfortunately, have low self-esteem. You do not think very highly of the things that you are capable of doing. You are afraid of opportunity and spend entirely too much time wondering about your inadequacies. You have a poor sense of timing and motivational skills. You thrive on being unhappy only to convince yourself that you can't do any better. None of this is true; you must know that you have a purpose and that your destiny is waiting for you. Change your attitude and get busy.

*Refer back to these exercises as often as you need to in order to remind yourself of your worth and what you were put on this earth to do. Your hope lies in Christ so always remember to rest in the promises of your Lord and Savior. Jesus gave his life for you before you were even conceived; therefore, your sins are forgiven and nothing can stop you from being who you were created to be. Your commission is to love God and to use your life to draw others to him. You have what it takes!

"And you shall love the Lord your God with all your heart and with all your soul and with all your mind and with all your strength." Mark 12:30

Glamour Girl Survival Tips

- Read The Entire Book of Esther.

- If you haven't already done so, join The Glamour Girl Movement at http://www.theglamourgirlmovement.com. You'll be the first to know about upcoming events, new videos from *The Glamour Girl Show* and so much more!

- Get connected with The Glamour Girl Movement on Facebook, MySpace, Twitter and YouTube!

  Facebook: http://www.facebook.com/theglamourgirlmovement

  MySpace: http://www.myspace.com/theglamourgirlmovement

  Twitter: http://www.twitter.com/ggmovement

  YouTube: http://www.youtube.com/GlamourGirlMovement

- Contact Megan at 1-855-GLM-GIRL for questions, comments, to leave a prayer request or share a praise report.

- Email megan@theglamourgirlmovement.com to request a Free 1-on-1 Beauty Consultation!

- Tell 5 Friends About The Glamour Girl Movement!

"I want to see you soar to greatness. I want to see you walk boldly in your purpose. Together we can be all that God has called us to be. I challenge you to experience The Glamour Girl Movement."

—Megan Mottley, Creator of The Glamour Girl Movement and
Author of *Glamour Girl: How To Get The Ultimate Makeover*

The B.E.A.U.T.Y. Sabbatical Experience

Beginning November 2011! Participate in a B.E.A.U.T.Y. Sabbatical with Megan Mottley.

First month FREE and only $19.99 per month thereafter for a beauty experience that will change you from the inside out! Join at any time! Go to **www.theglamourgirlmovement.com** to participate.

♦ Access to a Members Only site
♦ 1:1 B.E.A.U.T.Y. Evaluations each month
♦ Glamour Girl Power Calls each week
♦ FREE Glamour Girl Goodies from the B.E.A.U.T.Y. Chest
♦ Monthly Glamour Girl Reports

Notes

Unless otherwise noted, all Scripture references are from the King James Version of the Holy Bible.

American Heritage Illustrated Encyclopedia Dictionary, s.v. "remain."

Merriam-Webster's Collegiate Dictionary, 11th ed., s.v. "fear."

Nelson's New Illustrated Bible Dictionary, "Jewels and Precious Stones: Ruby." Thomas Nelson Publishers, 1995. 677.

Tanner, Gina. "Preparation of the Bride." *End Time Prophetic Vision* (2003). Accessed September 15, 2011. http://www.etpv.org/2003/prepo.html.

About The Author

Megan Mottley is the Founder of **MTLY Communications**, Publisher of **DIVINE Magazine**, Creator of **The Glamour Girl Movement** and Author of *Glamour Girl: How To Get The Ultimate Makeover.*

Megan has over 12 years of experience in the journalism industry and has worked in every facet of the media. Megan earned a Bachelor of Arts in English (specializing in Professional/Technical Writing) from the University of Memphis. She also earned a Master of Arts in Liberal Studies with an emphasis in Religion and Journalism from the University of Memphis. Megan received a professional license in Aesthetics from the Tennessee Academy of Cosmetology and for several years provided relaxation and rejuvenation services to salon clients and worked as a Freelance Makeup Artist. Megan is a 2009 graduate of Damascus Road, a ministry training internship and in 2010 she participated as a Mentee in Judy Jacobs' International Institute of Mentoring program.

Through her parent company, **MTLY Communications**, Megan provides consultation services that create professional and effective communication platforms for ministries, churches, non-profits, individuals, etc. Megan also motivates readers through her publication, **DIVINE Magazine**, a high quality print and digital Inspirational Magazine published quarterly since 2007. Megan has plans to transform lives through her newly created program, **The Glamour Girl Movement**, an inspirational experience designed to empower, ignite and rejuvenate women through beauty.

Megan is passionate about inspiring individuals to discover and walk boldly in their purpose. She believes that once a person understands the true reason for which they were created, the sky is the limit as to how they will impact the world.

MTLY Communications is a Multi-Media Company committed to motivating men and women globally through positive and inspirational Mass Media. Founded in 2007, MTLY Communications produces DIVINE Magazine, a high quality digital and print publication, which on a quarterly basis serves men and women by providing inspirational stories and features that encourage readers to discover and walk boldly in their purpose. MTLY Communications also has a publishing division, MTLY Publishing, which proudly produced *Glamour Girl: How To Get The Ultimate Makeover* and The Glamour Girl Movement. In addition, the MTLY Communications Consulting Division provides professional marketing and communications services. It employs Professional Writers and Editors with years of experience and a number of noteworthy clients. The MTLY Communications Consulting Division specializes in promoting the image of businesses, churches, ministries, and individuals with precision and excellence.

Utilizing 4 Components To Leverage You & Your Organization:
Media/Marketing. Trust. Leadership. You.
http://www.mtlycommunications.com
855.456.4475